The Better Covenant

The Better Covenant

*A 13-lesson Study
of the Book of Hebrews*

by
Milton S. Agnew

Beacon Hill Press of Kansas City
Kansas City, Missouri

Permission to quote from the following copyrighted versions of the Bible
is acknowledged with thanks:

The Amplified New Testament (Amp.), copyright 1958 by the Lockman
Foundation, La Habra, Calif.

The New English Bible (NEB), © The Delegates of the Oxford University
Press and the Syndics of the Cambridge University Press, 1961, 1970.
Reprinted by permission.

The Bible: A New Translation (Moffatt) by James Moffatt. Copyright 1954 by James Moffatt. By permission of Harper and Row, Publishers, Inc.

The Holy Bible, New International Version (NIV), copyright © 1973 by
New York Bible Society International.

New American Standard Bible (NASB), copyright © The Lockman
Foundation, 1960, 1962, 1963, 1968, 1971.

The Revised Standard Version of the Bible (RSV), copyrighted 1946,
1952.

Today's English Version of the New Testament (TEV), copyright ©
American Bible Society, 1966.

The New Testament in Modern English (Phillips) copyright © by J. B.
Phillips, 1958. Used by permission of the Macmillan Co.

The Living Bible (TLB), copyright © 1971, Tyndale House Publishers,
Wheaton, Ill. Used by permission.

The Modern Language Bible—the New Berkeley Version in Modern
English (Berk.), copyright © 1945, 1959, 1969 by Zondervan Publishing
House.

The New Testament in the Language of the People (Williams) by
Charles B. Williams. Copyright 1937 by Bruce Humphries, Inc., assigned
1949 to Moody Bible Institute, Chicago.

Contents

Preface

The Book of Hebrews is a penetrating study of the great doctrines of the Church as they originated in the Old Testament and as they are fulfilled and/or confirmed in the New. Of the search for these profound truths there can be no end. Excellent commentaries have appeared, and will appear, probing their depths with scholarly insight.

This volume is not intended to be such an in-depth treatment. (It was, of course, impossible in so short a time to cover every truth and plumb every depth.) Rather, it is a running account of what transpired in the author's class over a 13-week period as they studied together this profound Epistle. It is an attempt to reflect the observations of this group of thoughtful Christians, themselves not profound theologians but interested in exploring and clarifying for themselves some of these doctrines. We hope this presentation will be helpful to like-minded Christians— searching, earnest, practical.

The opportunity for discussion, for contribution, for research, for questioning was open from week to week. We tried not to be dogmatic where there was reason for a divergence of opinion, yet to be decisive where the Word was decisive. We had some differences of opinion but avoided contention. The summaries given herewith are a fair representation of the results of this process.

Members were encouraged to bring various Bible translations to class. Occasionally a commentary would appear. The blackboard, of course, was in constant use. In this volume some expansion of thought has been given, for in many cases this material could not be covered in the hour available. Scriptures quoted are from the King James

Version, except as otherwise noted. Italics have been inserted by the author for the purpose of emphasis.

We pray that this book may be meaningful, especially to the layman who follows the developing conclusions of those 13 weeks of study, and, hopefully, to the teacher who leads his own class in the study of the Word.

—MILTON S. AGNEW

God's Ultimate Message

By way of introduction, we noted that Hebrews was written to Jewish Christians of the first century who were faced with the understandably difficult task of accepting a reconciliation between the New Covenant and the Old. Indeed, they had trouble accepting the superiority of the New over the Old, but they were to discover how the Old is fulfilled in the New. To help them understand this, the author supplemented the actual *word better* with the *concept* of better. For example, through His Son, God presents a better revelation of himself (ch. 1). There is now revealed a better salvation (ch. 2). In Christ there is a better rest for God's children (chs. 3-4). In Christ there is a better hope (7:19), a better covenant (7:22); there are better promises (8:6), a better sacrifice (9:23), and a better resurrection (11:35).

We then noted that the Epistle very properly commences with a presentation of God's ultimate message. This is contained in the first three verses:

> God, who at sundry times and in divers manners spake in times past unto the fathers by the prophets, hath in these last days spoken unto us by his Son, whom he hath appointed heir of all things, by whom also he made the world; who being the brightness of his glory, and the express image of his person, and upholding all things by the word of his power, when he had by

himself purged our sins, sat down on the right hand of the Majesty on high *(Heb. 1:1-3)*.

In our examination, three great truths were brought out by the class, though not entirely in this order:

1. God spoke "in times past" by men.
2. God has now spoken "in these last days" by His Son.
3. God always has had a message for the world.

In an emphasis on the *pattern* of God's release of His message to the world "in times past," the writer begins his Epistle with two sonorous Greek adverbs, found only here in the New Testament—*polumerōs* and *polutropōs*. Being unique, and evidently having been very carefully chosen, these words carry a variety of translations. Those offered by NASB were finally chosen: "in many portions" and "in many ways" God spoke. Realizing that the Old Testament is made up of nearly 40 books, covering hundreds of years, we saw what the writer meant by "in many portions" (which the KJV translates "at sundry times").

We considered, for example, the revelations of a coming Redeemer. This, indeed, was fragmentary ("in many portions")—here a little and there a little. We listed some of them on the blackboard as the class suggested them, not necessarily in chronological order. There was God's great promise and disclosure to Abraham in Genesis 15 and elsewhere. There was the revelation to Isaiah that a virgin should bear a son (Isa. 7:14). There was the proto-evangelium of Gen. 3:15. There was the disclosure that the child would be born in Bethlehem in Mic. 5:2.

Then we examined the "many ways" or "divers manners" (KJV) used by God through the centuries of the Old Testament revelation. God spoke through the prophets by visions; He spoke face-to-face, from a burning bush, in the Psalms through nature. He spoke through religious symbols and ceremonies such as the sacrifices, the Day of Atonement, the garments of the priests, the Tabernacle.

It was noted that the first and second verses have the same subject—God. It was *God* who was speaking in times past through the prophets. It was *God* who had spoken again, now through His Son. Thus it is God—the *same* God—speaking in the Old and the New Testaments. His message is cohesive, consistent, comprehensive. God has always had a message for the world. He still has.

The second phrase, "in times past," reflected not only the previous years of His speaking, but also reflected, when Jesus finally came, the 400 years of God's silence since the last message had come from Him. We noted that some commentators see in the phrase "in these last days" (v. 2) evidence that "the author held to the belief that the End is now at hand." This, of course, may be true. But an examination of the Greek gives credence to the Amplified "in the *last* of these days," or the margin reading of NASB, "at the *end* of these days." This may well speak to the concluding sacrificial ministry of the days of our Lord, through which God's revelation through His Son was climaxed and concluded. In general the class preferred this interpretation.

We noted that there follows, in verses 2 and 3, a series of statements about the Son, indicating that He not only *brought* a message from God, but *was* himself the message from God.

First, God, in these last days, has spoken to us by His Son who, as "appointed heir" (v. 2) of all things, discloses the *provision* of God. For elsewhere (Rom. 8:16-17) it had already been recorded: "The Spirit itself [himself] beareth witness with our spirit, that we are the children of God: and if children, then heirs of God, and joint-heirs

11

with Christ." God's providential care for His own is ever evident.

Again, God has spoken to us by His Son who, as Creator—"by whom he made the worlds" (v. 2)—discloses the *purpose* of God. It was generally agreed by the class that to deny God's creative act leaves the world and mankind without any real purpose. But in the creation we see the purpose of God to provide himself with a people in His likeness, able to communicate and fellowship with Him, to worship Him. God works on a long-range plan.

Furthermore, God has spoken in these last days by His Son who, as "the brightness of his glory and the express image of his person" (v. 3), discloses the *character* of God. Again we found the various translations striving to do justice to the original Greek. "The effulgence of God's splendour and the stamp of God's very being" (NEB) was judged to be one of the better translations. But Moffatt's was also liked: "reflecting God's bright glory and stamped with God's own character." At any rate, what a disclosure of God's character was made in Christ! And that character is bright in its glory.

God has also spoken to us by His Son who, while "upholding" or sustaining all creation through "the word of his power" (v. 3), discloses the *orderliness* of God. We reviewed, for example, some of the amazing physical laws by which the universe is governed. Someone observed that the astronauts could not have been directed with such astonishing accuracy to a pinpoint landing on the moon except for the unvarying orderliness of God—"by the word of his power"! We also came to recognize that the physical laws are only representative of the unvarying and purposeful moral and spiritual laws with which He upholds mankind, and which, if disregarded, lead to chaos and oblivion. Indeed, "God is not the author of confusion" (1 Cor. 14:33).

Again, God has spoken in these last days by His Son

who, as the Purger of our sins, discloses both the *holiness* and the *mercy* of God. It had been centuries before, through the prophet Habakkuk, that it was declared, "Thou art of purer eyes than to behold evil, and canst not look on iniquity." To God sin was intolerable. But with God there also was mercy. He sent One to "purge our sins" (v. 3). In Jesus this God of purity *and* of mercy was to be seen as never before.

Finally, God has spoken in these last days in His Son who, as the restored Ruler of heaven, discloses the *majesty* of God. Jesus had "emptied himself" as He came in the likeness of man to be our Saviour. He now, having victoriously completed His mission, is set down "on the right hand of the Majesty on high" (v. 3). The sovereign majesty of God is epitomized in this imposing picture.

No longer did God speak in fragments, or in "divers manners." God's better message—indeed God's ultimate message—had come. God had spoken!

Lesson 2
Heb. 2:1-4

Nothing

The well-known answer to the question "What must I do to be saved?" is "Believe on the Lord Jesus Christ, and thou shalt be saved." The answer to "What must I do to be lost?" is "Nothing!"

Hebrews is dotted with numerous exhortations, warnings, and directives which apparently are thoughts of the writer in addition to the mainstream of his message. This is the first of these, contained in the second chapter.

> Therefore we ought to give the more earnest heed to the things which we have heard, lest at any time we should let them slip. For if the word spoken by angels was stedfast, and every transgression and disobedience received a just recompence of reward; how shall we escape, if we neglect so great salvation; which at the first began to be spoken by the Lord, and was confirmed unto us by them that heard him; God also bearing them witness, both with signs and wonders, and with divers miracles, and gifts of the Holy Ghost, according to his own will? *(Heb. 2:1-4).*

Members of the class quickly spotted the "therefore" and sensed that it referred back to the previous study in the first chapter. Since God has given a far greater revelation in the new dispensation in His Son than He gave "in time past unto the fathers" (1:1), certain responsibilities were laid upon those early Hebrew believers—and therefore upon us also, believers of today.

14

The scripture said, "We *ought* to give the more earnest heed." Other translations, we discovered, made this more emphatic with the word "must." For example, "We must pay more careful attention, therefore, to what we have heard" (NIV). It becomes an imperative.

"Lest at any time we should let them slip" seemed better translated "Lest we drift away from it" (NASB). Robertson says it is a metaphor "of being swept along past the sure anchorage which is within reach."

The writer gives a cogent reason for this compulsion. In the light of the fact that under the old, more primitive dispensation, every transgression, every disobedience "received a just recompence of reward, how shall *we* escape, if we neglect so great salvation . . . ?" under the new dispensation. The word "we" is emphasized in the Greek.

In discussing this greater responsibility laid upon those of the new dispensation, someone quoted Jesus: "For unto whomsoever much is given, of him shall be much required." Someone else reminded us that increased light must be obeyed: "If we walk in the Light, as he is in the light." Wesley is credited with saying, "Light obeyed increaseth light. Light rejected bringeth night."

Again, we noted that the writer called it a "so great salvation," i.e., a "better" salvation.

In looking for ways in which this salvation is greater, we identified four.

This salvation "at the first began to be spoken *by the Lord*" (v. 3). Jesus was the channel through whom it was first declared. Many of His sayings were quoted by the class members: "I am come that they might have life, and that they might have it more abundantly." "Ye must be born again." "For the Son of man is come to seek and to save that which was lost." "It is finished." "Seek ye first the kingdom of God, and his righteousness; and all these things shall be added unto you."

Again, this is a "so great salvation," says the writer, in that it "was confirmed unto us *by them that heard him*" (v. 3). Someone commented that perhaps the writer of Hebrews himself had not heard the Lord. That may be true. However, it did remind us of the importance of the witness of His immediate disciples. The Book of Acts is replete with such testimony, such confirmation. "Whosoever shall call upon the name of the Lord shall be saved." "Neither is there salvation in any other: for there is none other name under heaven given among men, whereby we must be saved." "And he commanded us to preach unto the people, and to testify that it is he which was ordained of God to be the Judge of quick and dead. . . . that through his name whosoever believeth in him shall receive remission of sins." Indeed, how great a salvation!

Again, we noted that the writer identifies the greatness of this salvation in that *"God also"* bore witness with them, "both with signs and wonders, and with divers miracles" (v. 4). It didn't take long for the class to recall and recount signs, wonders, and miracles wrought by Jesus through the power of God. The blind made to see, the deaf to hear, the lame to walk, the hungry to be fed, even the dead to live. Or was it the similar miracles by the disciples themselves through the power of God? Again, the lame man made to walk, the sick to be healed, prison doors to be opened. Whether through His Son or His disciples, *God* was endorsing this "so great salvation." Or do those signs and wonders and miracles refer to the healing of the spirit of man, the pardoning of his sins, the saving of the soul? The class rather preferred this latter thought.

Finally—and this seemed to us to be separate from the third instance—"God also bearing them witness . . . with . . . *gifts* of the Holy Ghost, according to his own will" (v. 4). We discussed the distinct possibility that the various gifts of the Spirit were here being referred to. As in

Corinth, the gifts of miracles, of prophecy, of the discerning of the spirits, of divers kinds of tongues. Or even more possibly the gift of "the more excellent way," the gift of love.

However, it was noted that in the original Greek the usual word for "gifts," *charismata*, is not used here, but rather the word *merismos*, literally "a distribution," "a bestowal." There appeared then to be a sound translation by Moffatt and by the marginal translation of NASB: "God also bearing witness . . . by *distributions* of the Holy Spirit according to His own will."

For, prior to this new dispensation, the Spirit was given only in special instances to only a few special people, who were called to special tasks. The Spirit was given to Gideon, Samson, and Saul, that they might deliver and rule His people; to skilled workers, that they might build the Temple; to a prophet, that he might speak for God to His people. But now, according to God's own will, in the new dispensation there were "distributions" of the Holy Spirit to many, indeed to all who sought Him. (Luke 11: 13). There was the distribution on the Day of Pentecost. There had been many others since to God's people when Hebrews was written. And, according to His own will, God *still* bears His own people witness to a "so great salvation" with distributions, bestowals, baptisms of the Holy Spirit upon them. This appears to be the ultimate of God's witness to this great salvation.

And woe to the man who neglects this salvation—so great and so complete!

In the light of this we questioned: What is the consequence which *we* who are Christians will not escape if we neglect?

In the old dispensation it had been "a just recompence of reward," "a due recompense" (NEB), "a just retribution" (RSV), "the punishment deserved" (TEV). In the new dispensation this of course may be a loss of fellowship, a sense of guilt, a stunted spiritual growth. But, knowing that the ultimate penalty of the old covenant was death, who are we to escape, under the new covenant, the deserved punishment of spiritual loss, of eternal death—if we ourselves neglect this great salvation?

The word "neglect" in NEB is "ignore." Phillips says, "refuse to pay proper attention." The same Greek word is used in Matthew 22:5 regarding those invited to the feast: "But they made light of it."

What must we who are saved do to lose our salvation? Neglect it; ignore it; refuse to pay proper attention to it; make light of it.

The Perfecting of Jesus

This mysterious and intriguing subject was a part of the total assignment of the second chapter of Hebrews. Here Christ is said to be superior to angels: first, in His message, vv. 1-4, which was considered last week; second, in His redemptive power, vv. 5-16, a portion of which we chose to consider this week; and third, in His priestly service, vv. 17-18, which will be considered later.

Our passage reads as follows:

> But we see Jesus, who was made a little lower than the angels for the suffering of death, crowned with glory and honour; that he by the grace of God should taste death for every man. For it became him, for whom are all things, and by whom are all things, in bringing many sons unto glory, to make the captain of their salvation perfect through sufferings. For both he that sanctifieth and they who are sanctified are all of one: for which cause he is not ashamed to call them brethren *(Heb. 2:9-11).*

We recalled that the writer in the first chapter had been showing how Jesus was superior to the prophets, and how in this chapter, superior to the angels. But here he proclaims that "for a little while" (NASB and other translations) he was made "*lower* than the angels."

Verse 9 is not easily translated. In considering several versions we finally decided that TEV was possibly the best expression of this truth: "But we do see Jesus! For a little while he was made lower than the angels, so that through God's grace he should die for all men. We see him crowned with glory and honor now because of the death he suffered."

This translation helped us to see *why* He was made lower than the angels. As God, Christ could not die, and therefore could not make an atonement for His people. Neither could an angel die for the people, nor make an atonement. But Jesus took on himself the nature of man, and as man was, for over 30 years, "lower than the angels." (See vv. 6-8.) Thus, as man he "tasted death for every man." He made atonement for man's sins. He became their Saviour.

And, "because of the death he suffered," He was again crowned with glory and honor. What an hour that must have been—the crowning hour of the returning Prince of heaven!

We then looked to the same translation for the tenth verse. "It was only right for God—who creates and preserves all things—to make Jesus perfect through suffering, in order to bring many sons to share his glory."

So, it was God himself—in desiring to make it possible for us, His "many sons," to share our Lord's glory—who "made Jesus perfect through suffering."

But what is meant by "making Jesus perfect through suffering"? The class agreed that He was never "imperfect" in His character, in spiritual purity, in respect to being sinful. So how did He need to be perfected? Someone referred us to Luke 13:32, where Jesus says: "Go ye, and tell that fox [Herod], Behold, I cast out devils, and I do cures to day and to morrow, and the third day *I shall be perfected.*" We found that the Greek verb used here is the same. RSV translates it "I shall finish my course." NEB and NASB "I shall reach my goal."

The words "the third day" then caught our attention. What "third day"? It was through His sufferings that Jesus, "on the third day," completed His course, reached His goal, was perfected. That third day must refer to His resurrection day. Indeed, only a *resurrected Lord* could be a Saviour. Paul said, "[Jesus] was delivered for our offences, and was raised again for our justification" (Rom. 4:25). And again, "If Christ be not raised, your faith is vain: ye are yet in your sins. Then they also which are fallen asleep in Christ are perished. If in this life only we have hope in Christ, we are of all men most miserable" (1 Cor. 15:17-19).

It was recalled that the chief cry of the new Church was "He lives," "He is risen," "Christ arose from the grave." Jesus himself had proclaimed, "Because I live, ye shall live also."

Furthermore, someone noted, it was the day of His resurrection, the "third day," that Jesus returned to His glory; He was again "perfected" as Ruler of heaven. He regained that of which He had emptied himself in His descent to the earth in His incarnation.

This was done, it says, that we might "share His glory." What does it mean to "share His glory"? To be praised and honored as gods? Hardly. To receive the obeisance of angels? We didn't think so. Then we looked to Paul's second letter to the Corinthians, chapter 3, verse 18: "But we all, with open face beholding as in a glass the glory of the Lord, are [being] changed into the same image from glory to glory, even as by the Spirit of the Lord."

In the following chapter Paul continues:

> For we preach not ourselves, but Christ Jesus [as] the Lord; and ourselves [as] your servants for Jesus' sake. For God, who commanded the light to shine out of darkness, hath shined in our hearts, to give the light of the knowledge of the glory of God in the face of Jesus Christ *(2 Cor. 4:5-6).*

This glory we share will be His glory shining out of our lives. We were helped in our understanding of this by examining the eleventh verse, again from TEV. "He makes men pure from their sins, and both he and those whom he makes pure all have the same Father. That is why Jesus is not ashamed to call them his brothers."

This verse told us that being made pure, being sanctified, brings His glory into our lives in a never ending cadence. We constantly are being changed from glory to glory—His glory, not ours.

It told us that the Sanctifier and the sanctified have the same Father. And it told us that Jesus is proud, then, to call us His brothers (and sisters). What a fellowship of holiness! Rich and poor. Educated and unlearned. Jew and Gentile.

One class member commented that this might have been quite a sobering thought to the Jewish believers of that day. For the Jews had always considered themselves to be God's chosen race, superior to the Samaritan, the Gentile, the uncircumcised. Now Jews could claim no racial superiority to other believers. "For both he that sanctifieth and they who are sanctified are all of one: for which cause he is not ashamed to call them brethren."

We thought of ourselves too. Don't we sometimes have a superiority complex when it comes to race? or education? or material possessions? We thanked God for a "better brotherhood" in Christ.

There Remaineth a Rest

The assignment for this day covered Heb. 3:1—4:13. There was in that day obviously an abiding danger that the Hebrew Christians would fail to enter a "rest" which was promised them. It is evident that the point of danger was "unbelief" (3:19; 4:11) or, as expressed in some translations, "disobedience."

This warning was raised from the example of the disbelieving, disobedient Israelites of Moses' day, who failed to enter the Promised Land of Canaan. This illustration would be an obvious one to the first-century Hebrews. But, since the Christians of today are likewise "the people of God" (4:9), there must be a word of warning as well as of promise to us as well.

Then, what was that "rest"? And what is it today?

In the light of those statements and questions we looked to the Word, reading this week from the *New International Version.* Hebrews 3:7-11 is a quote from the Ninety-fifth psalm:

> So, as the Holy Spirit says:
> "Today, if you hear his voice,
>   do not harden your hearts
> as you did in the rebellion,
>   during the time of testing in the desert,
> where your fathers tested and tried me,
>   and for forty years saw what I did.

> That is why I was angry with that generation,
>> and I said, 'Their hearts are always going astray,
>> and they have not known my ways.'
> So I declared on oath in my anger,
>> 'They shall never enter my rest.'"

This, we saw, would clearly be recognized by the Hebrews as the catastrophe which overtook the Israelites when they rebelled against God in the wilderness. Although they had been delivered from Egypt, they would not enter the promised "rest" of Canaan. The following words would be a stern warning to the first-century Hebrews:

> See to it, brothers, that none of you has a sinful, unbelieving heart that turns away from the living God. But encourage one another daily, as long as it is called Today, so that none of you may be hardened by sin's deceitfulness. We have come to share in Christ if we hold firmly till the end the confidence we had at first *(3:12-14, NIV)*.

We discussed this and realized that the warning was against becoming "hardened by sin's deceitfulness." Could Christians' hearts be so hardened? The writer of Hebrews evidently thought so.

Indeed he goes on to say in the fourth chapter:

> Therefore, since the promise of entering this rest still stands, let us be careful that none of you be found to have fallen short of it. For we also have had the gospel preached to us, just as they did; but the message they heard was of no value to them, because those who heard did not combine it with faith. Now we who have believed enter that rest. . . .

> It still remains that some will enter that rest, and those who formerly had the gospel preached to them did not go in, because of their disobedience. Therefore God again set a certain day, calling it Today, when a long time later he spoke through David, as was said before:

>> "Today, if you hear his voice,
>> do not harden your hearts."

For if Joshua had given them rest, God would not have spoken later about another day. There remains, then, a Sabbath-rest for the people of God; for anyone who enters God's rest also rests from his own work, just as God did from his. Let us, therefore, make every effort to enter that rest, so that no one will fall by following their example of disobedience *(vv. 1-11, NIV)*.

What is "his rest" (v. 1)? "that rest" (vv. 3, 6, 11)? "God's rest" (v. 10)? What indeed is a "Sabbath-rest for the people of God" (v. 9)? And what rest had Joshua failed to give the people whom he led into the Promised Land? These were perplexing questions.

We decided first of all that there *is* a greater—a better —rest promised God's people than the rest of the land of Canaan. That had been a rest from the rigors of the wilderness, from wandering, from homelessness. This rest probably was but a type of a greater rest—which rest Joshua was unable to give.

From verse 10 we might gather that this greater rest is a rest from "salvation by works." This indeed appears to be supported by Jesus in His great saying: "Come to me, all you who are weary and burdened, and I will give you rest. Take my yoke upon you and learn from me, for I am gentle and humble in heart, and you will find rest for your souls. For my yoke is easy and my burden is light" (Matt. 11:28-30, NIV).

The burdens imposed in that day by the Pharisees and scribes were intolerable—the burdens of the minutiae of the law, of tradition, of works. From this Jesus promised relief—rest.

Some in the class saw this as the true meaning of the rest offered. The Sabbath-rest for Christians must be a picture of ceasing from their labors, even as God did on the Sabbath day. Salvation was not to be by man's continuing works, but by God's completed work. "For by grace are ye saved through faith; and that not of yourselves: it is the gift of God: not of works, lest any man should boast" (Eph. 2:8-9). This certainly would apply to the first-century Hebrews, tempted to return to ritualism, to Judaism. But it applies to us also today, who might rely on self-effort for our salvation.

Others felt that God's rest meant simply a rest from worry, fretting, uncertainty, doubt. Too many Christians carry this burden. They need not. "Casting all your care upon him; for he careth for you." There is a "rest" provided by Christ from the burdens of the day, whether for the first-century Christians or for us of the twentieth century.

Then, someone suggested that the Canaan rest was but a type of a greater rest to come in the Christian's life. It was a type of a second crisis experience, the first having been depicted in their dramatic deliverance from Egypt. That had represented the sinner's deliverance from sins as found in salvation. As the Israelites had been delivered by faith, faith in the blood of the passover lamb, so are we delivered from our sinful lives by faith—faith in "Christ our passover . . . sacrificed for us." The Hebrew Christians had been through that crisis. They knew experientially the reality of a "so great salvation." This is the first great crisis experience for all believers.

But now, under the new dispensation, God desired to bring His people into the promised land of spiritual rest and plenty and peace. And this would come about through a second crisis experience known as sanctification, leading into the promised land of a holy life. It was available to the Hebrew Christians. It is available today to all believers. A life of purity. A life of being "more than conquerors" through Him that loved us.

This appeared to be an interesting and practical application. Into this rest, indeed, Joshua had not brought the children of Israel. It was left for another "today," inaugurated by another "Joshua," Jesus. (For it was noted that "Joshua" is the Hebrew form of the Greek "Jesus." For that reason it appears in KJV as "Jesus" in verse 8.)

Another example of typology, however, was explored: that this "rest" which "remains . . . for the people of God" is the eternal rest of heaven. It was recognized that there are Bible students who support this view. This may well be "God's rest"—the "Sabbath-rest for the people of God" (NIV). Surely that great day will provide a final, supreme rest for God's people, whether they be of the first or of the twentieth century.

Thus we found an interesting divergence of opinion in the class. And it did not seem wise to eliminate any one of the views as being unscriptural. But one thing remained in common. Whatever this "rest" may be, it can be forfeited, it can be missed, it can be rejected by a "heart of unbelief." God sternly warned these Hebrews of this possibility. And God warns us as readers of this same Epistle.

"Since the promise of entering his rest still stands, let us be careful that none of you be found to have fallen short of it" (NIV).

We then undertook what proved to be an interesting and rewarding research project. The hymnal of a church is a reflection of its theology. Since we were Salvationists we examined the Salvation Army official *Song Book* to see what was revealed in the use of the noun "rest."

We found, of the 1,017 songs, more than 40 using the noun "rest." None used this in a sense of rest from a "salvation by works." Probably this is because there are no such hymns, for certainly we would reject "salvation by works."

We did find several, possibly 10 or 12, which used the word "rest" in a general way, probably indicating rest from weariness, from worry, from fear, from uncertainty. These are represented by such verses as:

> *Beneath the Cross of Jesus*
> *I fain would take my stand,*
> *The shadow of a mighty rock*
> *Within a weary land;*
> *A home within the wilderness,*
> *A rest upon the way,*
> *From the burning of the noontide heat*
> *And the burden of the day.*
> > —ELIZABETH CECILIA CLEPHANE

> *I sighed for rest and happiness,*
> *I yearned for them, not Thee;*
> *But while I passed my Saviour by,*
> *His love laid hold on me.*
> > —B. E.

The use of "rest" to indicate an eternal heaven appeared in about the same number, represented by such verses as these:

> *O use me, Lord, use even me,*
> *Just as Thou wilt, and when, and where;*
> *Until Thy blessed face I see,*
> *Thy rest, Thy joy, Thy glory share.*
> > —FRANCES RIDLEY HAVERGAL

> *My rest is in Heaven, my rest is not here,*
> *Then why should I murmur when trials are near?*
> *Be hushed, my sad spirit; the worst that can come*
> *But shortens my journey, and hastens me home.*
> > —HENRY FRANCIS LYTE

We also found a common use of the word "rest" in songs listed under the "Holiness" section of the songbook, reflecting a "second blessing" experience. The following are samples:

> *I've wondrous peace through trusting,*
> *A well of joy within;*

This rest is everlasting,
  My days fresh triumphs win.

He gives me heavenly measure,
  Pressed down and running o'er;
O what a priceless treasure,
  Glory for evermore!
                              —JOHN LAWLEY

Just outside the land of promise
  You have waited many years,
And your life has been o'erclouded
  With a host of haunting fears.
There is victory in Jesus,
  Come to Him without delay;
Seek just now a full salvation
  And the voice of God obey.

Though you know your sins forgiven,
  Greater things await you still;
Freedom here from sin's dominion,
  Power to do the Master's will.
Fear no danger, He is with you,
  Let no foe your steps arrest;
Seek today the Father's blessing,
  Enter now the land of rest.

To redeem and make you holy
  Jesus left His throne above;
Now believe and take the blessing,
  Nothing less than perfect love.
                      —WALTER H. WINDYBANK

However, our analysis of the hymns of Charles Wesley proved of unusual interest. In his hymnody, of course, he particularly represents the holiness movement. And he does have great holiness songs centered on the word "rest." Consider the following:

O that I now, from sin released,
  Thy word may to the utmost prove,
Enter into the promised rest,
  The Canaan of Thy perfect love!

Lord, I believe a rest remains
  To all Thy people known,
A rest where pure enjoyment reigns,
  And Thou art loved alone.

A rest where all our soul's desire
  Is fixed on things above;
Where fear and sin and grief expire,
  Cast out by perfect love.

O that I now this rest might know,
  Believe, and enter in!
Now, Saviour, now the power bestow,
  And let me cease from sin.

However, his hymns interpreting this rest as pertaining to heaven are quite as prominent and numerous. Note these examples:

O may we thus be found
  Obedient to His word,
Attentive to the trumpet sound,
  And looking for our Lord!
O may we thus ensure
  A lot among the blest;
And watch a moment to secure
  An everlasting rest!

How happy every child of grace
  Who knows his sins forgiven!
This earth, he cries, is not my place,
  I seek my place in Heaven,

> *A country far from mortal sight;*
> *Yet, O by faith, I see*
> *The land of rest, the saints' delight,*
> *The Heaven prepared for me!*

Thus we came to the conclusion that our great hymn writers refuse to settle on one interpretation of the promised divine rest, applying it alike to the rest from worry and fretting, the rest from sin and sinning, the eternal rest of heaven. And who were we to be dogmatic in declaring that one precluded another? But we did feel that we now knew a little more about the rest that remains for the people of God.

In the closing paragraph of our assigned scripture, the writer is obviously referring to David's Psalm 95 as "the word of God," in which is outlined, with warning, the failure of the Israelites in Moses' day. He takes opportunity of using it as an example of the searching quality of God's Word:

> The word of God is living and active. Sharper than any double-edged sword, it penetrates even to dividing soul and spirit, joints and marrow; it judges the thoughts and attitudes of the heart. Nothing in all creation is hidden from God's sight. Everything is uncovered and laid bare before the eyes of him to whom we must give account *(vv. 12-13, NIV).*

In the light of all this he had urgently begged: "Let us, therefore, make every effort to enter that rest."

The Grace of God

We found in one brief excerpt from Hebrews 4 a plethora of truth, comfort, and exhortation—all centered in "the grace of God." Notice verses 14-16:

> Seeing then that we have a great high priest, that is passed into the heavens, Jesus the Son of God, let us hold fast our profession. For we have not an high priest which cannot be touched with the feeling of our infirmities: but was in all points tempted like as we are, yet without sin. Let us therefore come boldly unto the throne of grace, that we may obtain mercy, and find grace to help in time of need.

Here we found two urgent exhortations, separated by a profound statement of fact. We considered them in the order given.

"Let us hold fast our profession." As we compared various translations we found that the word "profession" is generally translated "confession." The Amplified helpfully says: "Let us hold fast our confession (of faith in Him)." Nevertheless, many of us felt that a "confession" was something admitted—often under pressure of evidence or circumstances and declared rather shamefacedly. We were reminded then of the passage in Rom. 10:9, "If thou shalt confess with thy mouth the Lord Jesus, and shalt believe in thine heart that God hath raised him from the dead, thou shalt be saved." And we discovered that Webster, although giving as his first definition "the act of disclosing one's sins to a priest," also declares that confession is "a formal statement of doctrinal belief." But some of us still preferred the KJV, "profession."

This profession or confession became the more pertinent when we examined the reason why we should hold it fast. "Seeing then that we have a great high priest, *that is passed into the heavens . . .*" we should hold tenaciously to our formal statement of doctrinal belief because we have a *risen* great High Priest. He is alive and in the presence of God, His Father.

Furthermore, we were being told that this profession does not automatically renew itself. Apparently there must be forces which would nullify it, steal it from us, cause it to be silent. What forces? Indiscriminate television viewing or reading, questionable worldly pleasures, an inordinate desire for money, things, and ease were proposed. Maybe the Hebrews of the first-century Church faced different destructive forces, like: Judaism, the pressures of a heathen community, the lack of writings comparable to those of the Old Testament to uphold and define their new faith.

At any rate, the elements of the human will, as a necessity for maintaining doctrinal belief, were recognized. Some suggestions were: a conscientious study of the great doctrines of the church, attending God's house, a life of prayer and communion, a bold witness to the unconverted.

We even mentioned some who apparently had forfeited this confession. From the Bible were mentioned Demas, Saul, Ananias. There were some whom we knew personally who had apparently forfeited it. We also admitted some regrettable memories of failure in our own lives.

Then we really became blessed as we considered the profound statement of fact in verse 15. We have a High

Priest in the heavens who understands us. Now Jesus as a *Prophet* spoke to the people on God's behalf, but as a *Priest* He spoke to God on behalf of the people. As our great High Priest He is our Intercessor "on the right hand of the Majesty on high." He is able to speak understandingly to God on our behalf, for He was "touched with the feeling of our infirmities" in that He was "in all points tempted like as we are."

We noted that the phrase "be touched with the feelings" is the translation of the Greek verb *sumpatheo*. *Patheo* means "to suffer," *sum*, "with." "Sympathize with," says NASB, NEB, and NIV; "feel sympathy with," says TEV. Angels could not sympathize with us. They were not subject to the suffering of temptations. We were even tempted to say that God himself could not really sympathize with us. For "God cannot be tempted with evil" (Jas. 1:13), but Jesus, "in the likeness of men" (Phil. 2:7), could be tempted—and was. Jesus, in His humanity, makes us better able to sense that He (and God His Father) *does* know how we feel. The Godhead cannot be divided. For "God was in Christ" (2 Cor. 5:19) as our Lord suffered His temptations. Thus at the throne of grace we find that sympathy, that understanding from both God the Father and God the Son.

"In all points tempted like as we are." There are three "points" of temptation, three basic areas common to mankind, and accommodating all temptation.

John lists them as "the lust of the flesh," "the lust of the eyes," and "the pride of life" (1 John 2:16). Eve had faced them in the Garden. "The woman saw that the tree was good for food, and that it was pleasant to the eyes, and a tree to be desired to make one wise" (Gen. 3:6). All temptation throughout the history of mankind has come under one or another of these three.

And our Lord "was tempted in all points like as we are." This is recorded in Luke 4.

First was "the lust of the flesh":

> And Jesus being full of the Holy Ghost returned from Jordan, and was led by the Spirit into the wilderness, being forty days tempted of the devil. And in those days he did eat nothing: and when they were ended, he afterward hungered. And the devil said unto him, If thou be the Son of God, command this stone that it be made bread (vv. 1-3).

Next, "the lust of the eyes":

> And the devil, taking him up into an high mountain, shewed unto him all the kingdoms of the world in a moment of time. And the devil said unto him, All this power will I give thee, and the glory of them: for that is delivered unto me; and to whomsoever I will give it. If thou therefore wilt worship me, all shall be thine (vv. 5-7).

Finally, "the pride of life":

> And he brought him to Jerusalem, and set him on a pinnacle of the temple, and said unto him, If thou be the Son of God, cast thyself down from hence: for it is written, He shall give his angels charge over thee, to keep thee: and in their hands they shall bear thee up, lest at any time thou dash thy foot against a stone (vv. 9-11).

So whether we are tempted by "the lust of the flesh," or by "the lust of the eyes," or by "the pride of life," we can comfortingly say, "You, Lord, understand. You were tempted in like manner."

There is an ominous implication in verse 13: "And when the devil had ended all the temptation, he departed from him *for a season.*" The implication is that the devil returned again. He did: in the person of Peter, when Jesus cried out, "Get thee behind me, Satan: thou art an offence unto me" (Matt. 16:23); in the Garden, when in agony of spirit Christ implored, "O my Father, if it be possible, let this cup pass from me: nevertheless not as I will, but as thou wilt" (Matt. 26:39); on the Cross, when "Jesus cried with a loud voice, saying, Eli, Eli, lama sabachthani? that is to say, My God, my God, why hast thou forsaken me?"

This may be borne out by the fact that the verb in Heb. 4:15 "was tempted" is not in the aorist tense, which would speak of a single act, of one instance, but in the perfect tense—"was tempted" in all points.

The perfect tense indeed speaks of one act, but it also speaks of a resulting state or condition. And this resulting state may be one of recurrent intervals of action like "The Father . . . *hath borne witness* of me [at recurrent intervals]" (John 5:37). Thus, our Lord *"was* in all points *tempted* [at recurrent intervals] like as we are" (Heb. 4:15).

However, as our example but unlike us, He was thus tempted, "yet without sin." He can remind us that sin can be resisted. In the light of this, John can write (1 John 2:1): "My little children, these things write I unto you, that ye sin not [at all]" (aorist tense—the tense of a single act).

What a message we found in the exhortation contained in the next statement! "Let us therefore come boldly unto the throne of grace."

Since we have a High Priest who can sympathize with us, we are urged to "come boldly unto the throne of grace." Why a throne and not an altar? or a temple? We decided it is because as Ruler of the universe He is seated there in judicial authority. We come to a throne. And we come boldly—not brashly, not brazenly, not presumptuously, but with a quiet confidence (RSV, NASB, NIV), with full assurance, with an untroubled heart, with courage (Williams), as came Esther before the throne of King Ahasuerus.

Reference to Young's *Analytical Concordance* gave us

still another facet to the word. It is *parrhēsia,* and may be translated "openly." John 18:20 records: "Jesus answered him, I spake openly to the world . . . and in secret have I said nothing." "Let us come *openly* to the throne of grace"—not in secret only (cf. Matt. 6:5-6).

At the throne we find grace in its two aspects: (1) the aspect of mercy, and (2) the aspect of help or assistance. The usual, acceptable definition for grace is, "the unmerited favor of God." But Webster also defines it as "divine assistance given man for his regeneration or sanctification." As a sinner, we come to find mercy. As a child of God, to find help or assitance. Both of these are contained in His grace.

The tenses of the verbs proved informative. These are not observable in any English translation, but quite apparent in the Greek. "Let us therefore come" *regularly,* again and again, to the throne of grace. For "come" is in the present tense of repeated action. We're always welcome at the throne.

We come as sinners "to obtain mercy" *immediately.* "Obtain" is in the aorist tense of an event, a completed transaction. There is no seriatim pardon of sins—one now and another later. They are all pardoned immediately in a complete transaction.

But, as the people of God, we come to the throne of grace "to find help" *again and again,* many times, frequently. "Find" is in that continuing present tense. And scholars tell us that Greek writers knew intuitively what tense to use in expressing an idea with accuracy; and certainly these writers would not be making changes recklessly. There is a significant reason for each change in tense to match a change in meaning. Thus the delicate, meaningful shades in this verse.

Illustrative of the promise that God's child, upon coming to the throne of grace, will find "appropriate help and well-timed help, coming just when we need it" (Amp.) is the following story by Lt. Col. Lyell Rader concerning a vivid experience of his missionary son-in-law:

Dr. Ted Gabrielsen was appointed to the small Salvation Army Hospital in Yong Dong, Korea. Only the shell of the building had survived the North Korean occupation. While various nurses and internes had tried to keep some medical work going, it had been without a Salvationist doctor for nine years. Everything stealable had been stolen, and the rest had rusted through.

Ted had great difficulty in impressing upon the Korean nurses the danger of handling penicillin carelessly. The drug had never been used here before. It is very effective germicide, but if the common staphylococcus germ is exposed to it in less than lethal doses, the germ becomes increasingly resistant to the drug at every doubling of its numbers, which takes place every few minutes by cell division. Thus, within a few hours, it becomes a veritable dinosaur, which cannot be killed by thousands of units. It is vital, therefore, not only that penicillin be used in adequate amounts to kill infection, but just as vital that every trace of it be cleaned up afterwards.

A New York State hospital had to be closed down because the "golden bug" had gotten loose, and had killed every baby in the nursery. The germ looks golden in color under the microscope.

Little wonder that a terrible staph infection broke out in the Yong Dong hospital. Before it could be identified, everyone in the hospital—patients and nurses— had it, including the doctor.

Ted frantically called his brother-in-law, Major Paul Rader, in Seoul, 130 miles to the north. "We've got the golden bug down here, Paul! Penicillin is totally ineffective at this point. Unless I can get some hexachlorophene within the next few hours, we'll at worst have some deaths, and at best I'll have to have one of my most important fingers amputated to save my own life, and that will be the end of my surgical career. Please hit every drug outlet in Seoul. If you can't get the pure drug, get Dial soap; it's loaded with it.'

A few hours later, Paul had to phone the heart-breaking news that no one had hexachlorophene, and they hadn't even heard of Dial soap. The bottom seemed to fall out of Ted's heart as he listened; but before he hung up, Paul said, "By the way, Ted, there's a box here with your name on it which came today."

Ted didn't have much interest in any more big boxes, although one miracle need after another had been supplied. "OK, pry it open and see what's in it."

Paul fairly screamed into the phone when he saw the contents. "Ted," he yelled, "it's Dial soap—a whole case of it!"

Ted shouted back, "You and Kay get your dunga-rees on and get down here as fast as you can. We'll give this place the greatest scrub dubbery it ever had in its life."

They lathered up the whole case and made poul-tices for the infections and scrubbed down everything that could have been contaminated. There were no deaths, and Ted did not lose his finger. They had prayed as they scrubbed, and wondered all the while where the soap had come from.

Months later, we discovered the source. The in-ventor of Dial soap had made an appointment to see the president of a chemical house. He arrived a little early, so he started to chat with the receptionist, and before long he brought up the virtues of his brainchild, this Dial soap. Just as the buzzer signalled to show him in, the receptionist (Colonel Rader's niece) said, "Say, if this stuff is so all-fired good, why not send a case of it to my cousin? He's a Salvation Army surgeon in Yong Dong, Korea."

He took time to note the name and address. That's all there was to it. Months later the case arrived *at the very moment of need.* Had it come a few weeks earlier, it would have been dissipated on ordinary chores. Had it been 24 hours later, it would have been too late. God's timing is always perfect. We have a new appreciation for Isaiah 64:25: "Before they call on me, I will answer; and while they are yet speaking, I will hear."

Lesson 6
Heb. 5:11—6:12

Perfection or Perdition

There are many people who *read* the Scriptures with conscientious regularity. But too few really *study* them. Too few follow the example of the Bereans (Acts 17:11) who "received the word with all readiness of mind, and searched the scriptures daily, whether these things were so." Our class was coming to realize that Hebrews is a book which challenges to real study.

Out of the fifth and sixth chapters arose a key question: Is spiritual maturity a *state* that one attains at a given point in his Christian growth, or is it a *process* of development that continues indefinitely?

"It's a process, and it should go on indefinitely" was the consensus. "Possibly there are plateaus attained somewhere, from which there can be further growth," added one thoughtful member. We decided we'd keep the question in mind as we studied.

The assignment covered Hebrews 5:11—6:12. This is another of the parenthetical exhortations and warnings which characterize Hebrews; not entirely related to what has just been said, but not unrelated either. The outline we followed was on the blackboard when the class opened:

1. A warning regarding continued spiritual immaturity (5:11-14)

2. An exhortation to spiritual perfection (6:1-3)
3. A warning regarding "falling away" (6:4-8)
4. An encouragement to persistence (6:9-12)

Actually, we never got to the last point, though of course it would have made a satisfying conclusion. For in it the writer speaks of his confidence in the Hebrew Christians, that *they* have not, and will not persist unto perdition. "Beloved, we are persuaded better things of you" (v. 9).

There is first the warning:

> Of whom we have many things to say, and hard to be uttered, seeing ye are dull of hearing. For when for the time ye ought to be teachers, ye have need that one teach you again which be the first principles of the oracles of God; and are become such as have need of milk, and not of strong meat. For every one that useth milk is unskilful in the word of righteousness: for he is a babe. But strong meat belongeth to them that are of full age, even those who by reason of use have their senses exercised to discern both good and evil *(Heb. 5:11-14).*

Out of this passage we gleaned two very pertinent truths. The first was that these Christians had among them some who were not only retarded ("Ye *ought* to be teachers"), they were retrogressive ("Ye have need that one teach you *again* which be the first principles"). These Christians had failed to profit by teaching which they had previously received. And again, ye "*are become* such as have need of milk, and not of strong meat." They had retrogressed from "solid food" to "milk." They were not attractive, *childlike* new Christian babes. They were unattractive (might we even say "repulsive," or at least "pitiable"?), *childish* Christians. And there *is* a difference.

That called for some observations on the characteristics which mark a childish Christian—pouting, selfish, easily offended, immature, emotional, unreasonable, undependable. Someone recalled the childish Corinthians whom Paul called "carnal Christians" (1 Cor. 3:1-3). They exhibited "envying," "strife," "divisions."

The second truth observed was that there *are* Christians who have become "of full age." They eat "solid food." They are those whose "perceptions are trained by long use to distinguish between good and evil" (NEB). They have achieved an age of spiritual responsibility and accountability. Thus he points out that Christian maturity *is* attainable in this life. Some of the Hebrew Christians apparently had attained it. Some had not. With those he would deal.

Then we turned to the exhortation in chapter 6:

> Therefore leaving the principles of the doctrine of Christ, let us go on unto perfection; not laying again the foundation of repentance from dead works, and of faith toward God, of the doctrine of baptisms, and of laying on of hands, and of resurrection of the dead, and of eternal judgment. And this will we do, if God permit *(vv. 1-3)*.

Out of this we gleaned two main areas of truth. The one was negative—regarding *foundations.* It is important that they be laid. It is also important that they be not torn up and relaid again and again. Someone likened this to starting the foundations over and over again so that the house never gets built. Or to planting corn and digging it up periodically to see if it has sprouted and is growing. "Not laying again and again [Greek] the foundation." Apparently laying and relaying these foundations is related to the "milk" previously referred to in 5:13.

There appeared to be three types of foundations. There are those in relationship to God—repentance and faith. There are those in relationship to the church in its rituals—baptism and laying on of hands. And there are those related to eschatology—resurrection and final judgment.

Each one of these the class considered important. We

discussed the frustrations in the lives of those who fail to establish sound foundations of repentance and faith, so they may "go on" from there.

The other area of truth was positive—regarding *progress.* Progress is normal, whether it be in the building of a structure, in the growing of a tree, or in the maturing of a Christian. "Let us go on" is a laudable and essential directive to Christian living.

Now, to make progress it is necessary to set a goal—the goal of "perfection," as the writer of Hebrews puts it. "But no one is perfect." "People would laugh at me if I told them I was perfect." "To expect perfection here would make Christianity impossible." "Probably we'll be perfect in heaven, but not here." Such were some of the comments on perfection.

But when we used other translations it seemed more possible—words like "maturity" (NEB, NASB, RSV, NIV); "adult understanding" (Phillips). An examination of Vine's *Expository Dictionary of New Testament Words* underscored this possibility. The word translated "perfection," he says, is "a fulfillment, a completion, an end accomplished as the effect of a process, stressing perhaps the actual accomplishment of the end in view."

It was informative next to learn that the adjective translated "that are of full age" (v. 11) is *teleios.* And that from this adjective is derived the noun *teleiotēs,* translated "perfection" in 6:1. The two words are close relatives. Therefore, if the adjective used in verse 11 describes actual people (as it obviously does), the noun used in verse 1 must describe an attainable goal. There is a reason and reasonableness in urging the retrogressive Hebrew Christians to go on unto the attainable goal of perfection or maturity.

The verb "let us go on" caught our attention. Research disclosed that it literally means "to carry" as in

Luke 23:26: "that *he might bear* it after Jesus." But here it is passive in mood, "be borne on," as in 2 Pet. 1:21: "Holy men of God spake as *they were moved* by the Holy Ghost." Our text then implies that there is a divine hand which, as we allow it, will bear us on to be mature adults—not babes but able to masticate solid food. *"Let us be borne on* unto perfection" is the encouraging admonition.

We noted that the preposition is "unto," not "towards." It is a goal that may be achieved, not just approached.

It was remarked that this "plateau" of adulthood should not mean stagnation. The Christian who is "of full age," who has reached "perfection," has a lifetime of growing, maturing, learning, and becoming more Christlike ahead of him. To this he must apply himself.

But now we turned to the second warning, given to those who fail to "go on." Continued retrogression will inevitably mean total loss.

> For it is impossible for those who were once enlightened, and have tasted of the heavenly gift, and were made partakers of the Holy Ghost, and have tasted the good word of God, and the powers of the world to come, if they shall fall away, to renew them again unto repentance; seeing they crucify to themselves the Son of God afresh, and put him to an open shame *(6:4-6).*

We knew we had in these verses a bundle of problems. One commentator says that this represents professed believers who, even after advancing to the very threshold of salvation, even after "going along with" the Holy Spirit in His work of enlightenment and conviction, halt short of faith in Christ. They never were saved.

Another says it is only a hypothetical case, for after he is really saved, he cannot actually fall away.

Another says it refers to believers who have fallen

into sin to the extent that they will lose their reward, though not their sonship.

Still another says that one may "taste" and not "swallow." They may have been members of the church but not of Christ.

Someone else sees in this the unpardonable sin.

In a complex sentence like this one, it is well to isolate the central statement. This appears to be: "It is impossible . . . if they shall fall away, to renew them again unto repentance."

In examining their credentials, we felt that the persons thus involved really were born-again Christians. They were once-for-all (Amp.) enlightened; they had tasted of "the heavenly gift . . . the good word of God . . . the powers of the world to come." And that "tasting" would be as positive as when Jesus "tasted death for every man" (Heb. 2:9). They were "made partakers of the Holy Ghost" just as truly as "we are made partakers of Christ" (3:14). Yes, the writer of Hebrews was speaking about genuine believers.

And he is also speaking about the real possibility of the apostasy of these genuine believers. The verb "fall away," *parapipto,* is unique to Hebrews 6. According to Vine *(Expository Dictionary),* it means "to fall away from adherence to the realities of the faith." Furthermore, "it is akin to the noun, *paraptoma,* 'a trespass,'" defined by him as "a lapse from uprightness, a sin, a moral lapse." It is frequently used, as in Eph. 2:1: "You who were dead in trespasses and sins." See also Matt. 6:14-15; 18:35; Mark 11:25-26; 2 Cor. 5:19; Col. 2:13.

The shocking corollary of this apostasy is that these persons are actually again crucifying Christ and holding Him up to shame. This, indeed, is intolerable to God. For Christ "has appeared once and for all at the climax of history to abolish sin by the sacrifice of himself. . . . So

Christ was offered once to bear the burden of men's sins" (Heb. 9:26, 28, NEB).

Does this mean, that a child of God, once having fallen away, can *never* be renewed again? Is this the unpardonable sin? Various translations seem to support this. NEB declares, "It is impossible to bring them again to repentance; for with their own hands they are crucifying the Son of God." NIV translates it: "Because to their loss they are crucifying the Son of God all over again and subjecting him to public disgrace." The *Living Bible* says: "You cannot bring yourself to repentance again if you have nailed the Son of God to the cross again."

An answer to the dilemma we found in the Amplified, and in the marginal reading of the NASB, supported by the Greek. "Seeing they crucify" is in the present participle form of the verb. It does *not* say, "Seeing they *have* crucified." Greek grammar will allow this to be a *causal* participle, as generally translated here: "seeing," "for," "because" they are crucifying. Grammar will also allow the present participle to be *temporal,* and be translated "while," "as long as" they crucify to themselves the Son of God.

The class immediately saw that this removed the hopelessness of the backslider. It is not just one falling away which seals the doom of him who falls away from his faith. It is only his *continued* apostasy which will accomplish that. "Seeing they crucify" is better translated "As long as they crucify." For, as soon as he ceased crucifying his Lord, as soon as he ceased putting him to open shame, then he could again "be renewed unto repentance." It was his choice.

The Hebrew Christians had been warned.

It was going on unto perfection or going back unto perdition. The choice was theirs.

And it still is.

Our Great Intercessor

"Intercession is entreating for another . . . it is prayer tuned to the needs of others . . . it is selflessness in our contact with God." These were some of the definitions volunteered by our class. Great intercessors of the Bible were recognized to include Abraham in his prayer for Sodom, Moses in his intercession for his people when they had sinned, Paul in his frequent prayers for his churches, the Church itself when it prayed for Peter in prison, and, of course, Jesus, particularly in His high-priestly prayer of John 17.

Recognition was also given to intercessors known to those of the class. The elderly and the shut-ins were mentioned particularly. "Lora was a woman who knew how to pray for others," one member observed, speaking with deep feeling of one who had just been promoted to glory that week. "She carried me over many a difficult place in my life. I'll miss her prayers for me."

The thoughts on intercession grew out of our reading of Heb. 7:25, "Wherefore he is able also to save them to the uttermost that come unto God by him, seeing he ever liveth to make intercession for them" (Heb. 7:25).

Again putting ourselves in the place of the Hebrew readers of the first century, we recognized the dual duties

47

of the high priest for his people, namely, making interces- sion and offering sacrifices. The particular attention here is on the former task.

On the blackboard we listed the following aspects of Christ's intercession and centered our discussion on them:

1. Its superiority
2. Its results
3. Its benefactors
4. Its authority

1. The *superiority* of His intercession was apparent when compared to that of the ordinary high priest. We noted that the writer had proclaimed Christ a Priest "after the order of" the mysterious Melchisedec (vv. 1-24). Without exploring the full historical background of this as outlined in the Old Testament (Genesis 14), we sensed that Hebrews is saying that Christ's intercession is thus superior to that of the priests, who had served the Israelites for these many centuries.

This superiority is thus in relation to position (vv. 9-10), since even Abraham payed tithes to Melchisedec and thus acknowledge his superiority. It is also in relation to timelessness (vv. 17, 21) in that Christ is thus a Priest, not for the brief span of a man's life, but "for ever." And that, for us, means *now,* in the twentieth century.

However, the superiority of His intercession relates not just to His being a Priest of this mysterious order, but to His being a High Priest of spotless character.

For such an high priest became us, who is holy, harmless, undefiled, separate from sinners, and made higher than the heavens; who needeth not daily, as those high priests, to offer up sacrifice, first for his own sins, and then for the people's: for this he did once, when he offered up himself. For the law maketh men high priests which have infirmity; but the word of the oath, which was since the law, maketh the Son, who is consecrated for evermore *(Heb. 7:26-28).*

When we listed some of the desirable characteristics of an effective intercessor—compassion, great faith, a burden, selflessness, spiritual insight—we decided that "godly" or "holy" or "close to God" really was the most important qualification. Only a person having this qualification could really pray effectively for another. This directly qualifies our Lord as our great Intercessor. He is holy, harmless ("innocent," NASB), undefiled, "separated" (NASB) from sinners.

And thus He "became us." This is in the rather colloquial language of saying that a hat or a dress are "becoming" to someone. "It was fitting we should have such a high priest" (NASB).

Furthermore, his intercession is based, not on daily sacrifices offered by the Aaronic high priest both for his own sins and also for the sins of the people, but upon a "once and for all" (NEB) sacrifice of himself.

2. The greatness of Christ's intercession is related also to the *results*. "He is able to save . . . to the uttermost" becomes "absolutely" in the NEB, "completely" in NIV and TLB, "throughout" in Berkeley. This spoke to us of the limitless *extent* of His saving grace through intercessory prayer. We knew this meant deliverance from the deepest and most penetrating sin. We knew this meant hope for the most profligate sinner. But we also recognized that it meant the unlimited heights to which His salvation would lift, the penetrating completeness of this salvation, the holy life to which He would commit those for whom He prayed.

As we compared various translations, we discovered that the phrase "to the uttermost" also became "for all time" in RSV, "forever" in NASB, "now and always" in TEV, and "for all time and eternity" in the Amplified. We thanked God for the "uttermost salvation" in *time* which His intercession also includes.

49

3. The greatness of Christ's intercession relates also to the *benefactors*—the recipients of His intercession ("them . . . that come unto God by him"—v. 25). It was suggested that this limits the benefactors to those who come "unto God," and to those who come "by him."

Limiting the benefactors to those who come "unto God" would be very acceptable to the Hebrew Christians. But to limit them to those who came *by Christ* might be more demanding to their faith. It is true that Jesus had said, "I am *the* way," and, "No man cometh unto the Father, but by me." It is true that the apostles had boldly declared soon after our Lord's sacrifice, "Neither is there salvation in any other, for there is none other name under heaven given among men, whereby we must be saved." But even so, this could be a real test to the faith of these first-generation Hebrew believers.

It was suggested also that this intercession is not only limited, but also limitless. For Jesus had said, "Him that cometh to me I will in no wise cast out" (John 6:37), and again of himself, "Whosoever believeth in him should not perish" (John 3:15-16). Everyone is invited to come to and by Him.

4. Finally, our Lord, as our great Intercessor, is endorsed by the *authority* of His intercession ("he ever liveth"). We turned our minds to the Hebrew Yom Kippur or Day of Atonement. We saw the high priest of the old dispensation, having made sacrifice for his people, making his awesome, annual entry, alone, into the holy of holies, there to make intercession for his people who waited without (Exod. 28:29). Someone in the class volunteered a legendary detail, new to most of us, but fascinating in its practical aspect. Since to enter this chamber unworthily meant death instantly, he had tied to his ankle a rope which extended outside. If he died, his body could be dragged out without endangering the life of another.

But he also had bells on his garment. His people listened intently as he moved about within. They heard the bells tinkling. "He lives," they murmured in awed thanksgiving, "he lives and prays for us." (See Exod. 28: 33-35.)

The great Intercessor! What a heritage is ours! Charles Wesley captured the theme in his well-known hymn:

> *He ever lives above*
> *For me to intercede,*
> *His all-redeeming love,*
> *His precious blood to plead;*
> *His blood atoned for all our race,*
> *And sprinkles now the throne of grace.*
>
> *My God is reconciled;*
> *His pard'ning voice I hear;*
> *He owns me for His child;*
> *I can no longer fear.*
> *With confidence I now draw nigh,*
> *And "Father, Abba, Father," cry.*

A Better Covenant

For centuries the Hebrews' pride was centered in their being "sons of the covenant" *(benai brith)*. This privilege was shared with no other people. In a marked sense the Jews felt that Jehovah belonged to them alone. And they were not noted as evangelists. (Jonah epitomized the reluctance of the Jew to become a missionary to the Gentiles.) God, they felt, had espoused the nation of Israel to himself as His bride. All others were "outsiders," "strangers." And now a "new" and "better" covenant? And that, to be shared with others? The very idea could be shattering to those first-century Jewish Christians.

The scripture upon which we anchored our discussion was Hebrews 8:6—9:24, the heart of which is 8:6: "Now hath he obtained a more excellent ministry, by how much also he is the mediator of a better covenant, which was established upon better promises."

We began our study by bringing together some basic facts about covenants.

First, what is a covenant? Is it a promise? A promise with a command? We finally agreed that a covenant is more than a mere promise. Indeed, it is a mutual promise or agreement between two or more parties. It bears joint responsibility. We examined business covenants and friendly covenants, but saw that the marriage covenant is possibly the best example. In fact, it has been used as a type of God's covenants with man both in the Old and the New Testaments.

We accepted the suggestion that it might be quite logical to divide the Bible into the Old and New *Covenants* rather than testaments. Someone recalled having seen a Bible so divided. We also discovered that some translations (NIV, NASB, TLB, Amp.) use the word "covenant" instead of "testament" in the passage under discussion. Some of these (NIV, TLB, Amp.) use "will" or "will and testament" in verses 9:16-17. A little research disclosed that, whether translated "covenant" or "testament" in KJV, the Old Testament Hebrew word *berith* was used many more times (260), than the New Testament Greek word *diathēkē* (33 times).

In case of a covenant between man and God, it is always God who initiates. However, man is required to respond and to continue to show responsibility. For example, the covenants made with Noah, with Abraham, with David, and the one made through Moses with the nation of Israel were named. As important as the other covenants might be, we finally agreed that the latter was the only one which could be compared with the New Covenant, and therefore the one to be identified as the Old Covenant. So we looked to "the book of the [old] covenant" (Exod. 24:7) for some facts about it as given in Exod. 20:1—24:8.

The book of the covenant outlines three types of law: ethical, judicial, and ceremonial.

The ethical code consists of the Ten Commandments (20:1-17). It was agreed that they were given to endure. They never have been repealed or withdrawn. However, they were immeasurably deepened and spiritualized by Christ (Matt. 5:21-48).

Then there is the judicial code, generally known as "judgments," commencing with chapter 21. These are judicial statutes outlining a code of behavior particularly related to that day and fulfilled in that day. The characteristic word is "if," marking hypothetical court decisions or judgments for those people under those circumstances. In their detail they were not to be perpetuated.

We also saw a brief summary of the ceremonial code as found in 23:14-19, outlining briefly three of the religious feasts or festivals which the Israelites were to observe—the Feasts of Unleavened Bread, of Harvest and of Ingathering. These and other festivals were to be fulfilled in Christ, in that they were types of Jesus and His ministry of sacrificial atonement. These are given in greater detail in Leviticus 23. These were not to be extended into the new dispensation either. They were finalized in Christ himself.

The sealing of the old covenant was interesting to observe, as recorded in Exodus 24 and recounted in Hebrews 9.

> And Moses came and told the people all the words of the Lord, and all the judgments: and all the people answered with one voice, and said, All the words which the Lord hath said will we do. And Moses wrote all the words of the Lord, and rose up early in the morning, and builded an altar under the hill, and twelve pillars, according to the twelve tribes of Israel. And he sent young men of the children of Israel, which offered burnt offerings, and sacrificed peace offerings of oxen unto the Lord (Exod. 24:3-5).

> Whereupon neither the first testament was dedicated without blood. For when Moses had spoken every precept to all the people according to the law, he took the blood of calves and of goats, with water, and scarlet wool, and hyssop, and sprinkled both the book, and all the people, saying, This is the blood of the testament which God hath enjoined unto you. Moreover he sprinkled with blood both the tabernacle, and all the vessels of the ministry. And almost all things are by the

law purged with blood; and without shedding of blood is no remission *(Heb. 9:18-22).*

The next step was to consider the characteristics which mark the new as a *better* covenant than the old.

We found it an exciting search.

1. *Better content.* The old was based on the letter of the law, which over the centuries became a complicated, cumbersome accretion of hundreds of commandments. The new was based on the spirit of righteousness (2 Cor. 3:6), related to the law of love (Matt. 22:34-40), upon which the whole new covenant rests.

> Not that we are sufficient of ourselves to think any thing as of ourselves; but our sufficiency is of God; who also hath made us able ministers of the new testament; not of the letter, but of the spirit: for the letter killeth, but the spirit giveth life *(2 Cor. 3:5-6).*

> Then one of them, which was a lawyer, asked him a question, tempting him and saying, Master, which is the great commandment in the law? Jesus said unto him, Thou shalt love the Lord thy God with all thy heart, and with all thy soul, and with all thy mind. This is the first and great commandment. And the second is like unto it, Thou shalt love thy neighbour as thyself. On these two commandments hang all the law and the prophets *(Matt. 22:35-40).*

2. *A better foundation.* While the old covenant was written on stone, indicating the stern and (necessarily) exacting righteousness of God, the new was to be put "into their mind, and written in their hearts" (8:10). It would represent the very *inner purpose* of the law of righteousness by the way of the intention, the will, the very purpose of the believer. Jesus had spoken to that (Matthew 5) when He had expressed His severe dissatisfaction with the outward, legal righteousness of the scribes and Pharisees (v. 20). With several illustrations He had outlined His own standards of inner righteousness.

3. *A better seal.* Both covenants are sealed with

blood. Indeed, it was noted previously in Heb. 9:18-22 that a covenant is not "dedicated" or initiated without blood, and that "without the shedding of blood there is no remission." Quite evidently the shed blood of these animals was pointing to the blood our Lord would shed to seal the new covenant, the second being of inestimably more value than the first. In this connection we read Matt. 26:26-28.

> And as they were eating, Jesus took bread, and blessed it, and brake it, and gave it to the disciples, and said, Take, eat; this is my body. And he took the cup, and gave thanks, and gave it to them, saying, Drink ye all of it; for this is my blood of the new testament, which is shed for many for the remission of sins.

4. *A better covenant partnership.* The old covenant was made with a people, the Israelites. Thus God would have a nation to whom He could entrust His "oracles," the Scriptures, and through whom He could make known His will for mankind. But the new covenant was made with individuals, with the person who would believe and commit himself and obey, whatever his national origin. "Whosoever" became the key word. And whosoever is always singular in the Greek language. His plan of salvation is one by one. "Whosoever" is also volitional. It imposes both a responsibility and also a possibility to every man.

5. *A better identification of the recipient.* Jewish boys were, by birth, "sons of the covenant," and technically only the male member of the nation could so qualify. Under the new covenant there was made a startling announcement, the like of which had never been made or even dreamed of under the old covenant: not "sons of the covenant" *(benai brith)*, but, by a new birth, "sons of God" *(tekna theou).* "As many as received him, to them gave he power to become *the sons of God,* even to them that believe on his name" (John 1:12). Nor is this limited to the

male only. For "there is neither Jew nor Greek, there is neither bond nor free, there is neither male nor female: for ye are all one in Christ Jesus" (Gal. 3:28).

6. *A better permanence.* There are two verses in the eighth chapter which speak of the first covenant by way of analysis and announcement:

> Had that first covenant been faultless, there would have been no need to look for a second in its place. But God, finding fault with them, says, "The days are coming, says the Lord, when I will conclude a new covenant with the house of Israel and the house of Judah." . . . By speaking of a new covenant, he had pronounced the first one old; and anything that is growing old and aging will shortly disappear *(8:7-8, 13, NEB)*.

It seemed strange to speak of the old covenant as faulty. But a further examination of it seemed to indicate that the faulty part of the covenant was the people with whom it was made. "But God, finding fault with *them* . . ." It was not that God had made "an error," but that the Israelites had failed. It takes two parties to make a covenant. Then, the covenant became "old," not in the sense that it was found to be decrepit but in the sense that it was both temporary and incomplete. That which was complete and permanent would, "in the fulness of God's time," succeed and supplant it. Thus the writer of Hebrews would identify this new covenant as "the everlasting covenant" (13:20).

7. *A better pattern.* The old covenant was represented by an intriguing and instructive Tabernacle, emphasizing the holiness, the eminence, the nearness yet exclusiveness of God, with a holy place accessible to the priest, and a holy of holies only to the high priest, and that once a year. The new covenant reveals all this as a type, fulfilled in a living Christ.

> The Holy Spirit is signifying this, that the way into the holy place has not yet been disclosed, while the

outer tabernacle is still standing; which is a symbol for the time then present, according to which both gifts and sacrifices are offered which cannot make the worshiper perfect in conscience, since they relate only to food and drink and various washings, regulations for the body imposed until a time of reformation. But when Christ appeared as a high priest of the good things to come, He entered through the greater and more perfect tabernacle, not made with hands, that is to say, not of this creation; and not through the blood of goats and calves, but through His own blood, He entered the holy place once for all, having obtained eternal redemption *(9:8-12, NASB)*.

For Christ did not enter a holy place made with hands, a mere copy of the true one, but into heaven itself, now to appear in the presence of God for us *(9:24, NASB)*.

8. *A better Intercessor.* As would be expected, reference was also made to the "better Intercessor" under the new covenant. (This was alluded to in the previous lesson.) "Wherefore he is able also to save them to the uttermost that come unto God by him, seeing he ever liveth to make intercession for them" (7:25).

A Better Sacrifice

This theme was supported by the section of scripture 9:11—10:14, but centered particularly on this verse: "It was therefore necessary that the patterns of things in the heavens should be purified with these; but the heavenly things themselves with better sacrifices than these" (9:23).

We explored first of all what was involved in a sacrifice. There was a feeling that there should be something "sacrificial" on the part of the one who gave it. It should be more than a passive gift or contribution. There must also be "an expression toward God." The sacrifice might relate to the forgiveness of sins, or to thanksgiving, or to worship. There should be a recognition of the inferiority and the dependency of him who offered it to Him who would receive it. In the case of atonement it would be a blood sacrifice. But it was recalled that the Old Testament sacrifices were sometimes those of grain or of fruit. We finally decided that, in the simplest terms, a sacrifice is a gift to God—a gift which has basic values to us and to Him.

As with the comparison of the covenants, we first looked at the nature of the earlier Old Testament sacrifices. We realized that up to the time of the destruction of the Temple in about A.D. 70, the sacrificial system was being continued in Jerusalem as the religious practice of the faithful. At the time of writing of Hebrews the Temple still stood. These Hebrews were still closely related to it by long association. It was through this they had received remission of their sins. It was in this that they maintained their position as sons of the covenant. It was in this practice that many of their own families still placed their reliance. Could they release the one and expect to find assurance in something entirely different? It would be a real test of faith.

The first recorded sacrifices appeared to be those of Cain and Abel (Genesis 4; Heb. 11:4), although there were members of the class who believed that sacrifice is implied in that God clothed Adam and Eve with coats of skins (Gen. 3:21). These, it is proposed, came from animals slain for sacrificial purpose. Although there is frequent mention made in Genesis of an altar being built—by Noah (8:20), by Abram (12:7; 13:4, 18; 22:9), by Isaac (26:25), and two instances of a sacrifice being made, both by Jacob (31:54 and 46:1)—still no system of sacrifices had been established before the time of Moses.

Indeed, the foundation of the old covenant was *obedience,* not atonement or atoning sacrifice. This is evident in the introductory remarks to the old covenant as recorded in Exod. 19:5: "Now therefore, *if ye will obey* my voice indeed, and keep my covenant, then ye shall be a peculiar treasure unto me above all people: for all the earth is mine."

This was reinforced by the words spoken at the sealing of the covenant as recorded in Exod. 24:3-7, the last verse of which says: "He [Moses] took the book of the covenant and read in the audience of the people: and they said, All that the Lord hath said will we do, *and be obedient.*"

Many years later, when preparing to announce God's

plan for a new covenant (Jer. 31:31-33), Jeremiah reminded the Israelites (7:21-23):

> Thus saith the Lord of hosts, the God of Israel; Put your burnt offerings unto your sacrifices, and eat flesh. For I spake not unto your fathers, nor commanded them in the day that I brought them out of the land of Egypt, concerning burnt offerings or sacrifices: but this thing commanded I them, saying, *Obey my voice,* and I will be your God, and ye shall be my people: and walk ye in all the ways that I have commanded you, that it may be well unto you.

Thus, when the covenant was broken in dramatic fashion by the Israelites in the making and worshipping of the golden calf (Exodus 32), *no pattern for an atoning sacrifice had yet been established.* Therefore there was the tragic retribution of the death of 3,000 men. It was in desperation, then, that Moses made his notable plea:

> And it came to pass on the morrow, that Moses said unto the people, Ye have sinned a great sin: and now I will go up unto the Lord; peradventure *I* shall make an atonement for your sin. And Moses returned unto the Lord, and said, Oh, this people have sinned a great sin, and have made them gods of gold. Yet now, if thou wilt forgive their sin; and if not, blot me, I pray thee, out of thy book which thou hast written *(Exod. 32:30-32).*

It was in the shadow of this deep, almost frantic concern by Moses that God renewed His covenant with His people (chap. 34), directed and observed the construction of the Tabernacle (chaps. 35—40), and established a system of sacrifices as recorded mainly in the Book of Leviticus. This included those sacrifices to be made for the atonement of sins.

For the Israelites, there were *daily* sacrifices (Exod. 29:38-44; Heb. 10:11) and *annual* sacrifices (Leviticus 23). The greatest annual festival and sacrifice, however, was

Yom Kippur, the Day of Atonement (Exod. 30:10; Lev. 16:1-30).

The principle of the sin offering was that, since death was the penalty for sin (Gen. 2:17; Ezek. 18:4; Rom. 5:12; 6:23), a life had to be given as a substitutionary death, and, if a life, then blood must be shed. Lev. 17:11 records this principle: "For the life of the flesh is in the blood: and I have given it to you upon the altar to make an atonement for your souls: for it is the blood that maketh an atonement for the soul." This, of course, was echoed in Heb. 9:22: "Without the shedding of blood there is no remission."

As it had been established by Abel, to be effective this sacrifice must be given by or in faith. Furthermore, repentance—a sorrow for sin and a sincere determination to forsake it and obey God—was also implied in the old covenant sacrifices.

We then investigated the word *torah,* the law, in which the sacrificial system is embodied. The basic meaning of this Hebrew word is "to throw"; hence, the meaning "to point out" (as by the throwing out of the hand). It is "direction." Thus the law, *torah,* was constantly a finger, pointing out, pointing forward, forward to something, to Someone. Thus the law was but a "shadow" (KJV), a "dim outline" (Phillips), a "faint outline" (TEV), a "foreshadowing" (Amp.), a "dim forecast" (TLB) of good things to come (Heb. 10:1). And those things came in Christ.

In the light of this background, we then searched Hebrews, mainly in chapters 9 and 10, for ways in which the new sacrifice was a better sacrifice. As before, we tried to see it through the eyes of the Jewish people to whom the letter was written.

1. This sacrifice was priceless, invaluable, costly. It was a sacrifice, not of the blood of goats and calves, but by His own blood. Heb. 9:12-14 reads:

Neither by the blood of goats and calves, but by his own blood he entered in once into the holy place, having obtained eternal redemption for us. For if the blood of bulls and of goats and the ashes of an heifer sprinkling the unclean, sanctifieth to the purifying of the flesh: how much more shall the blood of Christ, who through the eternal Spirit offered himself without spot to God, purge your conscience from dead works to serve the living God?

In the area of the value of the sacrifice, there certainly could be no comparison. Of course Peter (1:18-19) later gave further emphasis to this.

2. He offered himself. He died as He lived—purposefully. "How much more shall the blood of Christ, who through the eternal Spirit offered himself . . ." This, of course, agreed with our Lord's own statement, with which these Hebrew readers may well have had an acquaintance, since it later was recorded by John: "I lay down my life, that I might take it again. No man taketh it from me, but I lay it down of myself. I have power to lay it down, and I have power to take it again. This commandment have I received of my Father" (John 10:17-18).

But this was not so with the Old Testament sacrificial animals. They had no choice. They made no decision. They exerted no personal will.

3. As our Sacrifice, He died for us but He again lives. He is alive. This well may have come to us by the above statement by Jesus. But we found evidence for it also in these chapters of Hebrews, as in 9:24: "For Christ is not entered into the holy places made with hands, which are the figures of the true; but into heaven itself, now to appear in the presence of God for us." And 10:12 declares: "But this man, after he had offered one sacrifice for sins for ever, sat down on the right hand of God."

A Sacrifice who lives! This could be said of no animal

sacrifice. The sacrifice of the Old Testament spelled death. The Sacrifice of the New, life.

4. There was permanency in this new, better Sacrifice, and therefore in the goal it achieved—an "eternal redemption" (9:12). Under the old covenant the sacrifice had to be repeated daily, seasonally, yearly, thus achieving a redemption for a limited time. Who knew when his redemption ran out? It was like a short-term insurance policy, lapsing on brief notice. But this Sacrifice is featured by the word "once." And this "once" is not "once upon a time" *(pote)* as used by Paul in Gal. 1:23: "He which persecuted us in times past now preacheth the faith which once [upon a time] he destroyed." It is rather "once for all" *(ephax)* as we have it in Heb. 7:27: ". . . who does not need daily, like those high priests, to offer up sacrifices, first for His own sins, and then for the sins of the people, because this He did once for all when He offered up Himself" (NASB; see also NIV, RSV, NEB, TLB). And again, Heb. 10:10: "By that will, we have been made holy through the sacrifice of the body of Jesus Christ once for all" (NIV; see also KJV, NASB, RSV, NEB, TLB). It is "once for all" *(apax)* in 9:12 and 9:26 as well. (See NIV, NASB, NEB, RSV, TLB.)

Again, while it was with "many" sacrifices, year by year, the priests fulfilled their task, it was with "one sacrifice" (10:12) and "one offering" (10:14) our Lord fulfilled His task.

Surely the Hebrew believers must have been grateful for the orderly, eternal nature of their great Sacrifice and therefore of their great redemption!

5. Finally, there was a far greater efficacy in the new Sacrifice compared with the old. Chapter 10 reads in part:

> For the law having a shadow of good things to come, and not the very image of the things, can never with those sacrifices which they offered year by year con-

tinually make the comers thereunto perfect. For then would they not have ceased to be offered? because that the worshippers, once purged, should have had not more conscience of sins. But in those sacrifices there is a remembrance again made of sins every year. For it is not possible that the blood of bulls and of goats should take away sins. . . . By the which will we are sanctified through the offering of the body of Jesus Christ once for all. And every priest standeth daily ministering and offering oftentimes the same sacrifices, which can never take away sins: but this man, after he had offered one sacrifice for sins for ever, sat down on the right hand of God: from henceforth expecting till his enemies be made his footstool. For by one offering he hath perfected for ever them that are sanctified *(vv. 1-4, 10-14).*

The old sacrificial system could bring remission of, or forgiveness for sins (9:22). But it could not bring a deliverance *from*—a cleansing of—those sins (10:4, 11, 14). It could only bring a constant reminder to them every year of their sinfulness (v. 3). The sacrifices of the old dispensation could not lead on unto perfection (v. 1). We remembered the admonition in 6:1 that they not remain childish Christians, but "go on unto perfection." The sacrifices of the old covenant could not establish true sanctification. The sacrifices of the old may have *pointed* toward this, but they never provided the means for actual achievement.

But the new Sacrifice had. In Him the believer may, indeed, "go on unto perfection" (6:1; see 10:14), and that "by the one offering" and "for ever." His blood, His sacrifice "takes away sins" (9:26, 28); and by God's will "we are sanctified through the offering of the body of Jesus Christ once for all" (vv. 10, 14).

Indeed, as it never was, even to the greatest of saints of the old covenant, it is now "the privilege of all believers to be wholly sanctified." This must have been a startling revelation to these first-century believers. Although this they would know if they had contemplated the teachings of

Jesus. This they would know if they had studied the results of Pentecost.

6. A better body. This is related to an intriguing passage, 10:4-10, which has considerable importance in the total subject of "A Better Sacrifice." This passage presents God as dissatisfied with the sacrifice of the bodies of "bulls and goats" as the ultimate sacrifice. Therefore, He prepared for His Son a body, the body of a man. This human body served Jesus for the more than 30 years of His earthly life as the source of human life and vitality from which His ministry, His teaching, His example should flow forth, and in which He would be tried with all the temptations common to man. But ultimately, and actually primarily, it was to serve as the once-and-for-all Sacrifice for the sins of men.

It was the fulfillment of the typology of the old covenant, the ultimate to which the *torah* pointed through the centuries of its guidance. Only the sacrifice of *this body,* especially prepared by God for His Son, could give the ultimate cleansing from sin, the deliverance needed, the complete sanctification, the Christian perfection presented in this section.

The King James translation is very obscure. Several other translations, though accurate, are difficult to understand. We have therefore made an adaptation of *The Living Bible,* diligently comparing it with the Greek, using brackets to indicate the explanatory additions.

However, first, notice the footnote given in TLB to verse 4: "The blood of bulls and goats merely covered over the sins, taking them out of sight for hundreds of years until Jesus Christ came to die on the cross. There he gave his own blood which forever took those sins away."

Now note the text of Heb. 10:4-9 in TLB (with the above-mentioned emendations):

For it is not possible for the blood of bulls and goats really to take away sins. That is why [Christ] said, as he came into the world, "[O God], the blood of bulls and goats cannot satisfy you, so you have made ready this body of mine [for me to lay as a sacrifice upon your altar]. You were not satisfied with [the animal] sacrifices, slain and burnt before you as offerings for sin. Then I said, 'See, I have come to do your will, [to lay down my life], just as the Scriptures said that I would.'"

After [Christ] said this, about not being satisfied with the various sacrifices and offerings required under the old system, he then added, "Here I am. I have come [to give my life] [to do thy will, O God]."

He cancels the first system in favor of a far better one.

The King James Version concludes with the statement: "By the which will we are sanctified *through the offering of the body of Jesus Christ* once for all."

Lesson 10
Heb. 10:19-39

Greater Privileges
Bring Greater Responsibilities

The area under discussion during this session was verses 19-39 of the tenth chapter. It became quickly apparent that the writer was reminding the Hebrew Christians that their blessings, which were so much better than they and their forefathers had enjoyed under the old covenant, also brought greater accountability. There are grave warnings if these blessings should be abused.

Isn't that so with all of us? Jesus had said: "For unto whomsoever much is given, of him shall be much required: and to whom men have committed much, of him they will ask the more" (Luke 12:48). We reminisced regarding the increased responsibilities which had come upon us in life as we grew up.

The blackboard carried the outline:

1. Privileges and Responsibilities Under the New Covenant (10:19-31)

> Three Privileges
> Three Commands
> Three Duties
> Three Warnings

2. Encouraging Memories (10:32-34)
3. Further Admonitions (10:35-39)

Actually, the discussion majored on the four triads of point one. The writer did not accuse *them* of "drawing back unto perdition" (v. 39), but he gravely warns them not to "cast away their confidence" (v. 35). Then he brings them the frank statement by God himself, "My righteous one shall live by faith; and [but] if he shrinks back, My soul has no pleasure in him" (v. 38, NASB).

With that as a background, we then gave ourselves to the first section in its four triads.

1. *The Privileges*

As we studied these we again realized that God was talking through His servant to the Hebrews of the first century, and we tried to put ourselves into their place. But He was talking to us, too. The truths became very real to us.

The three privileges are marked by three "havings," indicating a present possession.

> Having therefore, brethren, boldness to enter into the holiest by the blood of Jesus, by a new and living way, which he hath consecrated for us, through the veil, that is to say, his flesh; and having an high priest over the house of God; let us draw near . . . having our hearts sprinkled from an evil conscience, and our bodies washed with pure water *(Heb. 10:19-22)*.

a. The first privilege was an astounding one—the right of entry into the innermost area of the tabernacle or temple. This was the area which, under the old covenant, was rigidly restricted to a once-a-year entry by the high priest. Any infringement on this as to person or time brought instant death. But now the believer had boldness so to do. What an astonishing thought!

Spiritualizing this, the writer was challenging every Christian that he now may have "boldness," confidence to come, *himself,* into the very presence of God. No longer must he depend on his representative, the high priest. *He* is welcome to the inmost fellowship with God. This he does, not with timidity, with apology, with fear, with apprehension, but with boldness entrusted to him by God himself.

When the Temple veil was rent from the top to the bottom at the death of Jesus, it was a symbol of the intimate accessibility of God to every believer. "By a new and living way," the scripture reads. We wondered if "way" should be capitalized—"Way." Hadn't Jesus identified himself as the Way (John 14:6)? And the early Christians been known as people of "the Way" (Acts 9:2; 16:17; 18: 25; 19:9; 22:4; 24:22)? This must have been a new and awesome thought to the Hebrew Christian who, all his life, had held the Temple to be very sacred and the holy place utterly inaccessible. It became an awesome thought to us also as we pondered upon our own rights in Him. That we— housewives, tradesmen, a merchant, a member of the police force, a retired Salvation Army officer—all have the right to enter into His very presence, with boldness!

b. Then, these early Christians were reminded that when they entered the holy place they would find there their own High Priest. He was alive and aware of their needs. Indeed, He was there to make intercession for them as needed. They would find a High Priest who is "holy, harmless, undefiled, separate from sinners, and made higher than the heavens." They would not come into the very presence of God alone, uninstructed, unnoticed, unannounced. And neither do we. The privilege of a Companion, a Champion of our cause, a Friend who understands, an Intermediary, is ours as well.

c. The third privilege spoke to the Hebrews undoubtedly of the twofold preparation—the sprinkling with blood, and the cleansing at the laver—which the priest observed who entered the Temple for religious ceremonies he was to perform. It would be interpreted in the Early Church, as it is now, that this entry into the very presence of God may be made boldly only by those who had pure hearts and clean hands (Ps. 24:3-4). They must be worthy. The familiar chorus came to mind: "He makes me worthy through His blood to walk with Him in white."

2. *The Commands*

The three commands or exhortations are characterized by the words "Let us . . ."

a. "Let us draw near with a true heart in full assurance of faith" (v. 22). Having entered the holy place, we must have full confidence to approach God into His very presence, since we have been "sprinkled" and "cleansed."

> *In the secret of Thy presence,*
> *In the hiding of Thy power,*
> *Let me love Thee, let me serve Thee*
> *Every consecrated hour.*

> *Saviour, dear Saviour, draw nearer,*
> *Humble in spirit I kneel at Thy cross;*
> *Speak out Thy wishes still clearer,*
> *And I will obey at all cost.*

> *I am Thine, O Lord; I have heard Thy voice,*
> *And it told Thy love to me.*
> *But I long to rise in the arms of faith,*
> *And be closer drawn to Thee.*

b. "Let us hold fast the profession of our faith without wavering; (for he is faithful that promised)" (v. 23). Don't panic under pressure. Don't doubt for a moment. Don't lightly cast away "the profession of your faith." He is faithful. Let us be likewise. The exhortation "Let us hold fast" suggested that there will be forces which will try to snatch away that profession. It was a new faith to the Hebrews—perhaps 30 or 40 years old at the most. Had it properly been proven in the rigors of life? Was it firmly grounded under a new dispensation? Were there not weaknesses being attacked by those who opposed it? Could they stand up under persecution?

Of course our faith, too, is attacked—by an unbelieving world, by a "liberal" education system, by the tragedies and burdens of life and by our own human limitations and weaknesses. The command to "hold fast" was most appropriate.

c. "Let us consider one another" (v. 24). How easily we can become self-centered. How easily we can treat others casually. The English word "consider" is the translation of the Greek word *katanoeō*. *Kata* in composition denotes "perfective" action, intensity. *Noeō* means to understand. This involves something more than surface, factual knowledge. It implies inward contemplation, a searching for the unseen significances. It has in it the aspect of evaluation, of respect. The combined word might be translated "consider carefully." It is used here and in Heb. 3:1: "Wherefore, holy brethren, partakers of the heavenly calling, *consider* the Apostle and High Priest of our profession, Christ Jesus." Were the Hebrews of the Early Church prone to be "inconsiderate" of one another? Of Christ himself? Are we?

It was instructive to note that all these exhortations of "let us" were in the present, continuing tense of uninterrupted action: "Let us consistently hold fast . . ."; "Let us regularly draw nigh . . ."; "Let us always consider one another . . ."

3. *The Duties*

a. The duty to mutual stimulation. "To provoke [one another] unto love and to good works" (v. 24). The Christian so privileged must stimulate others in a positive, constructive fashion, not provoking to anger, to jealousy, to despair, but "unto love and good works." The word "provoke" in the Greek has a sharp edge—for good or for bad. Paul and Barnabas had been separated by a "sharp *contention*" (Acts 15:39). Paul was so provoked *("stirred")* as he saw the city of Athens "wholly given over to idolatry" that he "preached unto them Jesus and the resurrection" (Acts 17:16, 18). God is looking for "provocative" Christians who will goad their fellow Christians on in the things of God. There were, evidently, and still are too many Christian nonentities.

b. The duty of Christian assembly. "Not forsaking the assembling of ourselves together, as the manner of some is" (v. 25). Evidently there had been persecutions (v. 33), which may have discouraged some in their attendance at church services. Maybe it was sheer carelessness. It might have been plain indifference.

We discussed the present-day tendency to irregular church attendance or even to nonattendance on the part of some professed Christians. We discussed the necessity today, especially as we "see the day approaching," to fortify one another by a regular "fellowship of the saints." The familiar story was recounted of the minister who visited the often-absent church member. A fire was burning on the hearth. Seeing his opportunity, the minister without a word removed one of the coals and set it aside on the hearth. Its glow diminished; it started to go out. The parishioner caught the significance. "I'll be there next Sunday," he promised.

c. Then there is the duty to mutual exhortation or, better, encouragement. "But exhorting [encouraging, NASB] one another: and so much the more, as ye see the day approaching" (v. 25). This faith was not an individual matter. Christians were to be interrelated and interdependent. They were to "consider" one another, to "provoke" one another, to "assemble" with one another, and now to "encourage" one another. Christians were not meant to be an island. They were meant to be part of a fellowship, an assembly, a church.

The "approaching day" came in for discussion. It might have meant the day of persecution. That came within the lifetime of many of those to whom he was writing. It may have referred to a day of cooling ardor and interest when the first fires of revival had died out. It may have referred to a day of discord within the church, or a day of material reverses for the members, or a day of temptation to return to Judaism. It was noted, however, that several translations (NIV, NEB, TEV) capitalize "Day," while *The Living Bible* frankly says "the day of his coming back."

4. *The Warnings*

We noted two or three things regarding warnings. They were not directed toward "them," the ungodly, the unsaved, the unbelievers, but toward "us" ("we"), the children of God. We are those who have been partakers of that full, experiential knowledge of the truth which Jesus identified with those who possessed life eternal (John 17: 3). We noted also 1 Tim. 2:4: "Who will have all men to be saved, and to come unto the knowledge of the truth."

The severity and specific nature of the warnings is also significant. Certainly they were not to be treated lightly. These new Hebrew Christians and we, today's Christians, must remember that.

a. The first warning is against the very possibility of apostasy. "For if we sin wilfully after that we have received the knowledge of the truth, there remaineth no more sacrifice for sins" (v. 26). This is a *presumptuous, a willful sinning,* not just an error in judgment, an act in ignorance. This is enlarged later to show planning, purposefulness, "with malice aforethought." Furthermore, it is a *continued practice,* not an isolated act. "If we sin" is a present participle. NIV accurately translates this: "If we deliberately keep on sinning."

b. The second warning is against the result of apostasy—judgment.

> . . . a certain fearful looking for of judgment and fiery indignation, which shall devour the adversaries. He that despised Moses' law died without mercy under two or three witnesses: of how much more sorer punishment, suppose ye, shall he be thought worthy, who hath trodden under foot the Son of God, and hath counted the blood of the covenant, wherewith he was sanctified, an unholy thing, and hath done despite unto the Spirit of grace? *(10:27-29)*.

c. The final warning is regarding the Executor of that judgment—God himself. "For we know him that hath said, Vengeance belongeth unto me, I will recompense, saith the Lord. And again, The Lord shall judge his people. It is a fearful thing to fall into the hands of the living God" (10: 30-31).

If these Hebrews were prone to take this new covenant lightly, to suppose that God's love and mercy would overlook carelessness or even impudence, or to feel a false sense of security once they were saved, then God severely checked that attitude right here. And maybe He *had* to be brutally frank and direct—as He may have to be with us.

Truly, *GREATER PRIVILEGES* do bring *GREATER RESPONSIBILITIES*—far greater!

A Better Faith

At first the eleventh chapter of Hebrews seemed isolated. For weeks we had been exploring the relationship of the new dispensation to the old through the eyes of the early Hebrew Christians. Christ was greater than the prophets, than the angels, than the high priest. The new covenant was better than the old, the new Sacrifice than the old. It is true that the vitality of "faith" had been introduced in the preceding verses (10:38-39). But still this chapter appeared to be a relatively unrelated though highly instructive discourse on faith.

It was probably the last two verses of the chapter which finally caught our attention: "And these all, having obtained a good report through faith, received not the promise: God having provided some better thing for us, that they without us should not be made perfect."

It had said in the second verse that "by it [their faith] the elders obtained a good report," or "received divine approval" (RSV). Now in these later verses the situation was summarized. In spite of this divine approval given these "heroes of the faith" through the centuries, they "received not the promise." But "we," the Hebrew Christians of the first century, (and of course the believers of the twentieth century) were recipients of that "promise," of that "some better thing," apart from which *they* could not be "made perfect." What was that "promise," that "better thing"? We have received what they anticipated.

The Living Bible helped in our search for the meaning of these verses: "And these men of faith, though they trusted God and won his approval, none of them received all that God had promised them; for God wanted them to wait and share the even better rewards that were prepared for us." What better rewards? The rewards of the new covenant? The rewards of the conquering Messiah? The rewards of the risen Christ? The rewards of deliverance from sin in sanctification? Could it be that *this* was what the "heroes of the faith," through the centuries, had been anticipating in their faith? And what was "the promise" that they received not?

We returned to the "elders," the "men of old"—Abel, Enoch, Noah. To what was their faith related? For *faith must have some revelation, some promise, on which it fastens.* What revelation or promise was theirs from God in that early day?

Someone in the class supposed it might be some unrecorded communication from God. Another ventured that it was regarding the type of offering God required from them. Someone else conjectured it might be a primitive form of the Ten Commandments which God had revealed in that pre-Sinaitic day. But then it was recalled that God's first revelation of His plan for redeeming the world—His first promise—was contained in Gen. 3:15, the so-called proto-evangelium or first gospel. This, indeed, was a sound and profound revelation on which these early men of God could ground their faith. "And I will put enmity between you [Satan] and the woman, and between your seed and her seed; *he shall bruise you on the head, and you shall bruise him on the heel"* (NASB).

A time was coming when the Seed (singular) of the woman (not of a man) should "bruise the head of Satan,

77

and in turn be bruised." It was agreed that, of course, the elders could not possibly have foreseen all the details of this prediction—a virgin birth of the Son of God in a Bethlehem stable; a period on earth of conflict between Him and Satan; His death on a cross "without the city gates"; His cry of triumph, "It is finished"; His resurrection the third day.

These details would only partially and gradually be revealed to the prophets through the centuries, and finally be displayed in Christ himself. But these, it appeared, were the "even better rewards" which they eventually were to share with us. This constituted "the promise" or "the better thing." *They* saw only the shadow. *We* now enjoy the substance. But it was quite obvious that their faith had been fastened to this primitive revelation from God.

We then examined one by one the accounts of faith under the old dispensation. "By faith [in the promise of the great Sacrifice] Abel offered unto God a more excellent sacrifice than Cain, by which he obtained witness that he was righteous, God testifying of his gifts: and by it he being dead yet speaketh." "By faith [in God's promise of ultimate victory over Satan and his kingdom] Enoch was translated that he should not see death." "By faith [that the child of the woman should, in God's own time, bruise Satan's head] Noah prepared an ark to the saving of his house." "By faith [in the revelation of a coming Saviour from sin] Abraham went out, not knowing whither he went." "By faith [in God's ultimate plan for victory] Jacob, when he was a-dying, blessed both the sons of Joseph; and worshipped, leaning upon the top of his staff." "By faith [in the promise of God's 'event' yet to come] Isaac blessed Jacob and Esau concerning things to come." "By faith [in God's promise of a 'seed' to the woman] Moses, when he was come to years, refused to be called the son of Pharaoh's daughter; choosing rather to suffer affliction with the people of God, than to enjoy the pleasures of sin for a season."

By faith in that basic revelation of final victory over sin which God had made in the Garden of Eden, Gideon, Barak, Samson, Jephthah, David, Samuel, the prophets "subdued kingdoms, wrought righteousness, obtained promises, stopped the mouths of lions, quenched the violence of fire, escaped the edge of the sword, out of weakness were made strong, waxed valiant in fight, turned to flight the armies of the aliens."

This was exciting. It seemed to belong. It knit together the entire chapter. It planted the chapter firmly among the accounts of "better things." Indeed, it related the faith of these Old Testament characters to the rewards (the "better things") enjoyed even then by the Hebrew Christians—and, we reminded ourselves, to the rewards enjoyed by us today.

If their faith in *promises* which were but shadows could so empower, so embolden and so encourage them, *how much more* should our faith in the *substance* of a crucified, risen Saviour empower, embolden, and encourage us. Their testimony, their witness (12:1) challenged us.

As we examined the particular events mentioned, we noticed also *particular* elements of revelation upon which the elders based their faith. Noah believed God's immediate warning "of things not seen as yet and was moved with fear." Abraham believed God's precise promise when asked to "go out unto a place which he should after receive for an inheritance . . . not knowing whither he went." And, when commanded to offer up his only son Isaac, Abraham also believed that "God was able to raise him up even from the dead."

Yes, there were many *particular* promises that they believed. But back of all of them was the belief in God—in a God who established a *basic, first,* and *final* revelation of promise.

It was recognized, too, that as the centuries progressed, further revelations from God were being made regarding the Seed of the woman. To Abraham, "In thee shall all families of the earth be blessed" (Gen. 12:3); to Moses, "I will raise them up a Prophet . . . like unto thee" (Deut. 18:18); through Isaiah, "Behold, a virgin shall conceive, and bear a son" (Isa. 7:14); and "But he was wounded for our transgressions, he was bruised for our iniquities: the chastisement of our peace was upon him; and with his stripes we are healed" (Isa. 53:5). These and many other revelations God was releasing, all relating to the first basic promise of God.

For the most part, however, these revelations, during the Old Testament years of the "heroes of the faith," were still shadows. The picture was veiled. Their faith of that day was placed in that which was far from being "perfected." "These all died in faith, not having received the promises, but having seen them afar off, and were persuaded of them, and embraced them."

Someone referred us to a feature of the *Thompson Chain Reference Bible,* "The Messianic Stars" (No. 4,221 in the chain). This provided material for a profitable search of the many promises in the Old Testament of the coming One.

In the closing moments of the class period we looked briefly at the introductory verses of the chapter, which some commentators accept as a definition of faith, and others insist is only a description of it.

There, largely by help of the NASB translation, we saw faith as the source of assurance, of conviction, of approval. We realized that it is by the same faith that we Christians accept the creationist "theory" as the authentic account of the beginnings of all. And that is not unimportant in these days.

Now faith is the assurance of things hoped for, the conviction of things not seen. For by it the men of old gained approval. By faith we understand that the worlds were prepared by the word of God, so that what is seen was not made out of things which are visible *(Heb. 11:1-3, NASB).*

What a revelation this eleventh chapter of Hebrews must have been to those early Hebrew Christians! Indeed, "God, who at sundry times and in divers manners spake in times past by the prophets, hath in these last days spoken unto us by his Son."

We sensed again our immense privilege—and responsibility—of living in this dispensation of "better things" which have been provided for us. And some day these elders of the pre-Christian centuries will share with us "the even better rewards that were prepared for us." The NEB seemed to sum it up well: "These also, one and all, are commemorated for their faith; and yet they did not enter upon the promised inheritance, because, with us in mind, God had made a better plan, that only in company with us should they reach their perfection" (Heb. 11:39-40).

Lesson 12
Heb. 12:1-17; 13:12

Sharing His Holiness

As we approached the end of the Epistle, we became particularly interested in what the writer would present as the pinnacle of his teaching. What would be the capsheaf of all these "better things" which had been unfolding week by week? It proved to be personal holiness of heart.

Our outline on the blackboard was as follows:

1. The *incentive* to holy living (Heb. 12:1-4)
2. The *discipline* of holy living
   a. God's discipline over us brings us to an *experience* of holiness (12:5-11).
   b. Our own discipline over ourselves brings a *life* of holiness (12:14-17).
   c. Christ's supreme act of self-discipline *makes possible* this holiness for His people (13:12).

The NASB brought clarity to this chapter, and we used it as the translation for this lesson.

> Therefore, since we have so great a cloud of witnesses surrounding us, let us also lay aside every encumbrance, and the sin which so easily entangles us, and let us run with endurance the race that is set before us, fixing our eyes on Jesus the author and perfecter of faith, who for the joy set before Him endured the cross, despising the shame, and has sat down at the right hand of the throne of God *(vv. 1-2).*

Three things we are exhorted to do: to "lay aside," to "run with endurance," to "fix our eyes."

Now the great cloud of witnesses, whom we had examined in the preceding chapter, seemed to be not so much witnesses who watched, but witnesses who testified. They testified by their overcoming lives that they had been victorious because they had "laid aside," had "run with endurance," and had "fixed their eyes." In their great admiration for their national heroes of the past centuries, the Hebrew Christians were urged to emulate them. The emphasis is on "us also."

In trying to understand their hindrances, we did some confessing as to those which beset us today. Our list on the blackboard came to be something like this:

Besetting Sins	*Weights*
Temper	Laziness
Jealousy	Recreation
Inordinate pride	TV
Indifference	Worry

We found that the two were not very far apart. Weights could easily become sins. Some weights were not a hindrance in moderation. Some sins might more properly be called weights.

However, someone noted that the besetting or entangling sin is singular—"the sin." What might be a besetting sin threatening all God's children? We decided that, since the common *asset* of the fathers was "faith," the common besetting *sin* might well be lack of faith, doubt, faithlessness. And might this not be the besetting sin today of believers? Be that as it may, the Hebrew Christians were encouraged to lay aside, with the fathers of old, "every encumbrance," and that "sin which entangles."

Then consider the endurance and patience of the great men of old. There was Enoch, who walked with God alone; Noah, who preached for 120 years with no converts; Abraham, who waited almost 100 years for the heir promised him; Moses, who bore the trials of a recalcitrant people across a wilderness for 40 years. Let "us also" run with endurance the race that is set before us!

We liked the expression "fixing our eyes on Jesus" in NASB better than "looking unto Jesus" in KJV, especially when we discovered it to be a rare verb in the Greek, used only twice in the Scriptures, and meaning "to look away from all else and fix one's gaze upon." The writer had carefully chosen his words. The heroes under the old covenant had looked in faithful anticipation, while those of the new covenant looked in happy realization.

Actually, our incentive to holy living was seen to be twofold—(1) the example of the "witnesses"; (2) our own constant and persistent view of our Saviour and Lord.

We then turned to the second section of our outline: "The *discipline* of holy living." This is the "discipline" center of the Bible. In no other place is the subject so thoroughly covered. We found it declaring three things.

1. *Discipline is needful.* "All discipline for the moment seems not to be joyful, but sorrowful; yet to those who have been trained by it, afterwards it yields the peaceful fruit of righteousness" *(12:11, NASB).*

Were the Hebrews chafing under Christian discipline? Having divested themselves of the requirements of the law under the old covenant, were they not "free" and unencumbered under the new? No, they were not, but this discipline "afterwards yields the peaceful fruit of righteousness."

2. *True discipline from God is, as from a father, given in love.*

You have forgotten the exhortation which is addressed to you as sons,
"MY SON, DO NOT REGARD LIGHTLY THE DISCIPLINE OF THE LORD,

NOR FAINT WHEN YOU ARE REPROVED BY HIM;
FOR THOSE WHOM THE LORD LOVES HE DISCIPLINES,
AND HE SCOURGES EVERY SON WHOM HE RECEIVES."
It is for discipline that you endure; God deals with you
as with sons; for what son is there whom his father does
not discipline? But if you are without discipline, of
which all have become partakers, then you are illegiti-
mate children and not sons *(12:5-8, NASB)*.

And what are the disciplines of our Father, given in
love? Suffering and sickness? Bereavement? Sometimes
poverty? Loneliness? Restrictions and regulations regarding conduct? Yes, all these seem to apply. Someone suggested temptations, and then changed it to testings. For
God does not tempt us to do evil. But "allowing us to be
tempted" was accepted, for did not God allow Job to be
tempted by the devil?

But we decided His disciplines are not all "sorrowful"
or "grievous." There were the positive disciplines of His
commandments, His teaching, and His example. For the
Greek word *paideuō* speaks not only of punishment, but
also of instruction. "And Moses *was learned* in all the
wisdom of the Egyptians, and was mighty in words and in
deeds" (Acts 7:22). See also Acts 22:3, "taught"; and 2
Tim. 3:16, "instruction."

3. *God's discipline is superior to that of an earthly
father.* This is in view of the eternal and supreme purpose
involved.

Furthermore, we had earthly fathers to discipline
us, and we respected them; shall we not much rather be
subject to the Father of spirits, and live? For they dis-
ciplined us for a short time as seemed best to them, but
He disciplines us for our good, that we may share His
holiness *(vv. 9-10, NASB)*.

That last phrase in the KJV reads, "That we be partakers of his holiness." What a rewarding discipline God
exerts! This holiness was not just to be admired or merely
revered as sacred and unapproachable. It was not just to

be desired, or to be studied. No! It was to be shared *with Him,* even as a man shares a meal with his family. Using the same verb NASB declares of the Early Church that "they were *taking* their meals *together* with gladness and sincerity of heart" (Acts 2:46).

This was an application of the previous exhortation: "Having therefore, brethren, boldness to enter into the holiest by the blood of Jesus . . . let us draw near with a true heart in full assurance of faith" (10:19, 22). The Hebrew Christians were learning something of their amazing privileges and provisions in Christ.

And now, what of *self-discipline?* We saw it in verses 14-16:

> Pursue after peace with all men, and after the sanctification without which no one will see* the Lord. See to it that no one comes short of the grace of God; that no root of bitterness springing up cause trouble, and by it many be defiled; that there be no immoral or godless person like Esau, who sold his own birthright for a single meal *(NASB).*

In examining the strong Greek verb translated "pursue after," we realized it was much more appropriate than the "follow" of the KJV. Pursuit requires discipline—indeed, *is* a discipline. The enjoyment of peace and sanctification is worthy of concentrated effort, and in fact demands it. Peace with all men is listed as a common pursuit along with purity before God. The Hebrews needed to sense that God's holiness which they are to share with Him is not only heavenly and eternal, but is also earthly and present. This holiness belongs not only in a sacred holy

---

*This is the "see" *(horaō)* of comprehension rather than sight. As a blind man would say, "Oh, I see what you mean." It was used of Jesus, "When he *saw* their faith" (Mark 2:5); by Jesus, "Blessed are the pure in heart: for they shall *see* God" (Matt. 5:8); by Peter, "For I *perceive* that thou art in the gall of bitterness" (Acts 8:23).

place, but also in the marketplace, in the workshop, in the home. It related to their attitude toward all men.

We also examined the warnings that follow under the heading of "See to it" or "looking diligently" (KJV) and recognized this to be self-imposed discipline: "See to it that no one comes short of the grace of God; that no root of bitterness springing up cause trouble, and by it many be defiled; that there be no immoral or godless person like Esau, who sold his own birthright for a single meal" (vv. 15-16, NASB).

There is the warning against "coming short of," "missing" (NIV), "failing" (KJV), "forfeiting" (NEB) God's full grace in one's life; the warning against the possible inroads of bitterness or jealousy of spirit; the warning against the infiltrating of actual sin into the household of God. These all call for stern self-discipline by the child of God.

As a parenthesis we examined verse 17: "For you know that even afterwards, when he desired to inherit the blessing, he was rejected, for he found no place of repentance, though he sought it with tears" (NASB).

In this translation and in the KJV, it is not clear what Esau sought so diligently. Some translations unfortunately indicate that he sought vainly for a place of repentance. However, "it" is feminine in gender and requires a feminine antecedent. "Place" is masculine and will not do. However, "blessing" is feminine, and the NIV has therefore translated the verse: "Afterward, as you know, when he wanted to inherit the blessing, he was rejected. He could bring about no change of mind, though he sought the blessing with tears."

It was the stolen "blessing" Esau was interested in. He cared not for repentance. His tears were not tears of repentance, but of frustration and petulant anger.

But of supreme interest is the greatest self-discipline of all—that of our Lord, declared in chapter 13, verse 12: "Therefore Jesus also, that he might sanctify the people with his own blood, suffered without the gate." These Hebrew Christians already knew that Christ had suffered for their *sins,* that they might be *saved* (Heb. 9:22, 28). They must also know that He died for their *sinfulness,* that they might be *sanctified.* And that this is the price He paid that they might "share His holiness."

We realized that the Hebrews of the first century would know their Greek, in which language this letter was written so we scanned these verses to discover what to them would be plain.

In English the verb tense speaks to us of the *time* of action—past, present, future. The Greek spoke to them in tenses which indicate not only the time but also the *type* of action. The "present" tense, for example, indicated to them a continuous or repeated action, like an endless line. The aorist tense, however, spoke to them of an individual act, a completed transaction which occurred at a given time, like a point in time. If there was a change from one tense to another, it was *always* done purposefully.

This aorist tense of an isolated act or crisis experience appears in important places, sometimes in a surprising way. For example, look again at the verse before us: "Therefore Jesus also, that He might [at a point of time] sanctify the people through His own blood, [at a point of time] suffered outside the gate" (NASB). This sanctification, then, was to include a crisis experience to the believer, accomplished because of a crisis experience by their Lord.

Back in 12:1, the aorist tense was used. The writer commands, "Let us also lay aside [at a point of time— right now] every encumbrance, and the sin which so easily entangles us" (NASB). The believer must not dally with his besetting sin or with the weights that hinder. He is to make it a matter of urgent business, to be accomplished in full, if he is to run with patience the race set before him.

Then there is verse 10: "That we may share his holiness." Surprisingly, this too is in the aorist tense. The Amplified has caught the significance of this as a crisis experience in translating it: "That we may become sharers in His own holiness."

On the other hand, we learned that the continuous present tense of continued action governs the admonition "let us run" and the definition "fixing our eyes on Jesus." Furthermore, it exhorts to persistence in the verbs "pursue after" and "see to it." The holy life is one of continuous self-discipline.

Summing it up, through the act of His suffering Jesus has provided the crisis experience of sanctification, which is to be followed by a day-by-day pursuit and restraint. Holiness is thus a growing and ever continuing experience, built upon a decisive act of faith.

Times of Transition

These Hebrew Christians were yet in grave danger. There was the danger of drifting back into Judaism as found in chapters 8—10. Recall, for example, 9:8-10:

> The Holy Ghost this signifying, that the way into the holiest of all was not yet made manifest, while as the first tabernacle was yet standing: which was a figure for the time then present, in which were offered both gifts and sacrifices, that could not make him that did the service perfect, as pertaining to the conscience; which stood only in meats and drinks, and divers washings, and carnal ordinances, imposed on them until the time of reformation.

This statement of danger is repeated in this last chapter. For there was also the real danger of their drifting back into atheism, godlessness, and sinfulness. Recall the warnings of chapter two regarding neglect. Remember the grave warning of chapter 3:12, "Take heed, brethren, lest there be in any of *you* an evil heart of unbelief, in departing from the living God." And be mindful of the earnest warning in chapter six to those who might "fall away" if they *continued* to "crucify to themselves the Son of God afresh, and put him to an open shame."

However, this final chapter seemed mainly to be an assortment of brief exhortations. Indeed, they might well be an enlargement of the writer's directive recorded in 12:

14, "Pursue after peace with all men, and after the sanctification without which no one will see the Lord" (NASB). They comprise practical applications of the directive to holy living.

Since the writer seems to present his material somewhat at random, we then tried some form of organization of the thoughts contained. We came up with this:

1. Friendly attachments (vv. 1-2, 5-6)
2. Relationships to others (vv. 3-4, 7, 17-19)
3. Matters of doctrine (vv. 8-16)
4. Postlude (vv. 22-25)
5. The great benediction (vv. 20-21)

The theme "friendly attachments" stems out of the fact that the Greek word *philos* makes up a part of three separate words found in the three indicated areas. Standing by itself as a noun, it will be translated "friend," as in Luke 7:6 ("The centurion sent friends . . ."). As a verb it may be second in importance to Christian love, *agapaō*. It describes a highly respected attitude of loving with emotion and warm friendship. Jesus thus loved Lazarus (John 11:4), and indeed the Father thus loves His Son (John 5:20). In composition, as we will see, *philos* is again usually, but not always, a desirable emotion and attitude.

"Brotherly love" (13:1) attaches the word for brother, *adelphos,* to make the interesting *philadelphia.* The writer is encouraging a continuation of warm friendship and wholesome emotion between brothers. This could well include brothers of the same physical family, but quite apparently enlarges the scope to embrace the spiritual family of the church. It is a praiseworthy relationship, both for that early Hebrew assembly, and also for any church of today. Warm friendship should mark every assembly of believers. It is part of the fellowship we should have "one with another."

In verse 2 the word for "stranger" *(xenos)* is used in

composition to make *philoxenia. The Living Bible* has aptly translated it, "Don't forget to be kind to strangers." How closely related is kindness to friendliness. This Christian friendship was not to be limited to "brothers" in Christ but must reach out to the stranger. How aptly may this admonition be applied to any church of today! We concluded that the "stranger" was the person of another race, the newcomer, the neighbor who never goes to church; indeed, the ungodly and unruly of the community.

"For thereby some have entertained angels unawares." Was the writer thinking of Abraham and the angels he entertained, one of whom proved to be the Lord himself (Genesis 18)? Was he thinking of our Lord's own statement, "Inasmuch as ye have done it unto one of the least of these my brethren, ye have done it unto me" (Matt. 25:40)?

The third use of *philos* in a composite word is in verses 5 and 6. Here it is even more obscure to casual perusal. It is found in the words "without covetousness" or "free from the love of money" (NASB). *Arguros* means "money," or, more literally, "silver" (Matt. 10:9). Then *a* as a prefix indicates negative. Thus the Greek word appears *aphilarguros,* "without a love of money." Had money a deteriorative influence even then? Evidently Paul thought so, in that he used the same word, without the prefix, to declare, "For the love of money is the root of all evil" (1 Tim. 6:10), or as the NASB has it, "of all sorts of evil." (See also NIV, TLB.)

Does this mean that one should be content with his wages? someone asked. We decided that contentment did not thwart ambition, and that legitimate temporal needs had to be met. But contentment did counter covetousness. For covetousness speaks of desire for something which rightly belongs to another—like another man's house, his automobile, his wife, his money. Besides, we came to see the warm assurance of *His* presence and of *His* unfailing help. That spells contentment. What does Paul say in that same letter to Timothy? "But godliness with contentment is great gain" (6:6).

We then turned to the area of "relationship to others." The verses concerned have in common some word which allies us to those about us.

> *Remember* them that are in bonds, as bound with them; and them which suffer adversity, as being yourself also in the body *(v. 3)*.

> *Remember* them which have the rule over you, who have spoken unto you the word of God: whose faith follow, considering the end of their conversation *(v. 7)*.

> *Obey* them that have the rule over you, and submit yourselves: for they watch for your souls, as they that must give account, that they may do it with joy, and not with grief: for that is unprofitable for you. *Pray for* us: for we trust we have a good conscience, in all things willing to live honestly. But I beseech you the rather to do this, that I may be restored to you the sooner *(vv. 17-19)*.

As previously indicated, there are four separate admonitions under this heading.

1. The first two would deal with a fault common to many—forgetfulness. There were those in trouble. "The prisoners," says NASB, "as though in prison with them; and those who are ill-treated, since you yourselves also are in the body." Could "them that are in bonds," "the prisoners," also mean those bound by sin, the prisoners of habits? Could those who "suffer adversity" also mean those who are ill, poverty stricken, under great tragedy? How should we "remember them"? In prayer? In practical service? In friendly concern?

2. "Remember your leaders," declares the NIV (v. 7), "who spoke the word of God to you. Consider the outcome of their way of life and imitate their faith." Then this

translation adds in the same paragraph, "Jesus Christ the same yesterday and today and forever" (v. 8). We found this interpretation meaningful, as the second admonition against forgetfulness.

We did remember some of our leaders. We recalled their admonitions from the word of God, their "way of life," "their faith." Being mature people, we all had recollections of "the leaders of yesterday." It did us good to give them honor and to thank God for them. Then we thanked the writer of Hebrews for reminding us that Jesus Christ has not changed. He will perform the same marvellous works of grace today, possibly through us; possibly through those presently bearing the burden of leadership; possibly through the young people coming up in the Lord's work.

3. The third area of "relationship to others" spoke about obedience and submission to those who "must give account" (v. 17). We liked the way *The Living Bible* expresses it: "Obey your spiritual leaders and be willing to do what they say. For their work is to watch over your souls, and God will judge them on how well they do this. Give them reason to report joyfully about you to the Lord and not with sorrow, for then you will suffer for it too."

4. The fourth aspect of relationship was in prayer. Phillips expresses it well in verses 18 and 19: "Pray for us. Our conscience is clear before God, and our great desire is to lead a life that is completely honest. Please pray earnestly, that I may be restored to you the sooner."

The first-century readers would be aware of what we learned, that the tense of each of these verbs of encouragement—"remember," "obey," and "pray"—was the present tense, the tense of continued, uninterrupted performance. The writer was reminding these first-century Christians that God had a right to expect consistency in their attitudes and practice.

There is one other verse dealing with interpersonal

relationships in a very intimate way: "Marriage is honourable in all, and the bed undefiled; but whoremongers and adulterers God will judge" (v. 4).

It is to be noted that in KJV the verb "is" is in italics, indicating that it really is not in the original text. Thus NASB, and other later translations, have chosen to render it as an exhortation: "Let marriage be held in honor among all, and let the marriage bed be undefiled; for fornicators and adulterers God will judge."

The matters of doctrine, verses 9-16, constitute the final statement on this subject. These include a further warning and instruction to the Hebrew Christians, then final directions. The first part (vv. 9-12) reads as follows from NASB:

> Do not be carried away by varied and strange teachings; for it is good for the heart to be strengthened by grace, not by foods, through which those who were thus occupied were not benefited. We have an altar, from which those who serve the tabernacle have no right to eat. For the bodies of those animals whose blood is brought into the holy place by the high priest as an offering for sin, are burned outside the camp. Therefore Jesus also, that He might sanctify the people through His own blood, suffered outside the gate.

The "varied and strange teachings" may have been those of Judaism; the "foods", the culinary restrictions observed by the Jews. Don't again "be carried away" with them. In them there is no real profit. One wonders if they were beset by as many "varied and strange" doctrines as are we! They had an altar, but we have a greater, a better altar—the cross of Jesus Christ!

Geographically, Calvary was "outside the gate" of Jerusalem. Theologically, Jesus suffered "outside the camp" of Judaism, to establish a new order, a better covenant.

In the early days of the Church, believers worshipped

with the Jews in the Temple (Acts 3:1; 5:42; etc.) and in the synagogue (Acts 9:20; 13:14; etc.) But, now, later in the century, it became apparent that Christianity must break away from Judaism, going "outside the camp."

> Hence, let *us* go out to Him outside the camp, bearing His reproach. Here we do not have a lasting city, but we are seeking the city which is to come. Through Him then let us continually offer up a sacrifice of praise to God, that is, the fruit of lips that give thanks to His name. And do not neglect doing good and sharing; for with such sacrifices God is pleased *(vv. 13-16, NASB)*.

There appears to be here a fourfold duty for this young church: sanctification (v. 12), separation (v. 13), habitation (v. 14), dedication (vv. 15-16).

It is this last chapter, and particularly the postlude, which changes the complexion of Hebrews from being a dissertation to being a personal epistle.

> And I beseech you, brethren, suffer the word of exhortation: for I have written a letter unto you in few words. Know ye that our brother Timothy is set at liberty; with whom, if he come shortly, I will see you. Salute all them that have the rule over you, and all the saints. They of Italy salute you. Grace be with you all. Amen *(vv. 22-25)*.

But it was in the magnificent beauty of the benediction which precedes this that we bade farewell to the Book of Hebrews. We didn't discuss it, any more than you would dissect a rose to enjoy its beauty. We just accepted its blessing:

> Now the God of peace, that brought again from the dead our Lord Jesus, that great shepherd of the sheep, through the blood of the everlasting covenant, make you perfect in every good work to do his will, working in you that which is well-pleasing in his sight, through Jesus Christ; to whom be glory for ever and ever. Amen *(vv. 20-21)*.